These two wise women unpack
relationship addiction—with piercing h
dose of common sense and practical ste
thinks they need a partner to be happy in life, this book is a lifeline.

Katherine Woodward Thomas

New York Times bestselling author of *Calling in "The One"*

This is an important book. Sherry Gaba clearly identifies a common pattern in relationships and shows the negative results on relationships of self-abandonment.

Margaret Paul, PhD

Co-Creator of Inner Bonding

When Sherry talks I listen. Why? Because she brings together what she has learned from her personal recovery with her rich clinical expertise and experience and shares with us her deep wisdom. This book on relationships is a must read for anyone who wants to find a way to better connect with someone they care about.

Allen Berger, PhD

Author of *Love Secrets: Revealed; 12 Stupid Things that Mess Up Recovery; 12 Smart Things to Do When the Booze and Drugs Are Gone; 12 Hidden Rewards of Making Amends; 12 More Stupid Things that Mess Up Recovery*

Sherry Gaba has taken her already ground-breaking work on sobriety and codependency to new depths with this book. In my thirty years of recovery, I've seen relationship addiction destroy almost as many lives as substance use disorders. The two are not unrelated. The rigorous yet compassionate approach introduced by Sherry will support scores of women to recognize and begin to resolve their deadly obsession with marriage, love, and relationships.

Dawn Nickel, PhD

Creator, She Recovers

This is a book that explains in detail why so many of us marry without knowing our motivations or those of the other person involved in the relationship. It further shows the reader the importance of understanding that continually repeating your actions with no satisfaction is what addiction is all about. Sherry Gaba and Beth Adelman have joined together to present the reader with a book that is so badly needed in today's society, where we all seem to be seeking pleasure without understanding the consequences of our choices. Together, they have gracefully presented their own experiences to demonstrate how easy it is to become a relationship junkie, and how to free yourself from continuing to be one. This book is a gift to all of us who are seeking a healthy intimate relationship. It is a must-read.

Joan S. Peck

Author of *Prime Threat—Shattering the Power of Addiction*

Relationship addiction is seldom discussed, but is a crippling problem for so many who believe they are nothing without a partner. Sherry and Beth explore the roots of this addiction and offer a practical, empathetic, honest path to understanding, healing, and living fabulously on your own. This book is for everyone who thinks they need a partner to be happy.

Sunny Dawn Johnston

Speaker, teacher, and author of *The Love Never Ends* and other books

Sherry and Beth look at relationship addiction, where it comes from, what drives it, and what can be done to break free, with honesty, empathy, and a huge dose of common sense. This book is for everyone who thinks they need a partner to be happy, or wants to know how to heal from past pain, live fabulously on your own, or choose the partner you truly deserve.

Dr. Ava Cadell

Author and founder of LoveUniv.com

This is a thoughtful and generous book. Sherry Gaba's honest and insightful examination of the negative patterns in her own life offers hope to readers that they can escape the negative patterns in theirs.

Ethlie Ann Vare

Author of *Love Addict: Sex, Romance and Other Dangerous Drugs*

Sherry Gaba is a gifted recovery personality who so generously and candidly shares from her own experience in this latest book. As both a professional and as someone who has struggled with many of the issues highlighted in the book, I trust Sherry's voice on these delicate subjects very much. The book, if approached with an open mind and open heart, will help you to do your own work and to grow in your healing and recovery.

Jamie Marich, PhD

Clinician, Trainer

Author of *Trauma and the Twelve Steps; Trauma Made Simple; Dancing Mindfulness; EMDR Made Simple; EMDR Therapy & Mindfulness for Trauma-Focused Care*

Full of warmth and wisdom, psychotherapist Sherry Gaba's new book is a valuable resource for anyone who is constantly looking for the "perfect" relationship. She offers practical advice for breaking the cycle of relationship addiction and shows readers how to build inner security and peace of mind.

Beverly Conyers

Author of *The Recovering Heart; Everything Changes; Addict in the Family*

If you're ready to transform your love life, you need to read this book! With equal parts honesty and empowerment, Sherry Gaba shines a light on our addictive behavior in relationships. Best of all, she teaches us how to create the changes we want to make.

Lisa Sue Woititz

Author of *Unwelcome Inheritance: Break Your Family's Cycle of Unhealthy Behaviors*

Sherry Gaba's new book is an important read for the "relationship junkie." Do you find yourself obsessing over a love interest or repeatedly experiencing extreme, frequent ups and downs in your marriage, marriages or relationships? By sharing personal and client experiences, Sherry helps readers understand relationship addiction and its root causes. She then provides a series of exercises to help readers determine the nature of their relationship obsessions, as well as steps and suggestions for creating the space in which they can heal and finally stop the vicious cycle.

Lisa Frederiksen

Author, speaker, trainer, consultant

Founder of BreakingTheCycles.com and SHDPrevention.com

This book introduces the new concept of "relationship addiction." Written with compassion, Sherry Gaba's style is engaging and easy to read. She describes the cycle of pain that relationship addicts suffer, which she herself experienced. The book delves into the causes and offers healing solutions.

Darlene Lancer

Author of *Codependency for Dummies; Conquering Shame and Codependency*

This book is a must-read for anyone struggling with relationship issues, or for anyone who wants a great education on relationship dysfunctions. Sherry does a great job painting a clear picture of relationship dysfunction and gives the reader practical suggestions to deal with their issues. Anyone who reads this book will benefit tremendously!

Rosemary O'Connor

Certified life and addiction coach

Author of *A Sober Mom's Guide to Recovery*

Many confuse obsession and care-taking with true love. Sherry Gaba does an excellent job of pointing out how they are different. She invites the reader to not only stop and look at their behavior patterns, but guides the reader through the tangles of pseudo-relationships to find an intimate relationship with heart.

Brenda Schaeffer

Author of *Is It Love or Is It Addiction?*

We create relationships in our lives to fully study and express the issues within ourselves that need to be addressed. In Sherry Gaba's new book, she explores this truth and leads you to discover what you need to address personally, as opposed to "what is wrong with them." In the final analysis, most couples come together to explore the same issues from different perspectives. When they both can be objective enough to realize this, real change can be experienced.

Dee Wallace Channel

Author, actress, speaker

Sherry Gaba has written a powerful and yet easy to read book on the prison of relationship addiction. The book takes the reader through the sources and causes of this type of addiction. Unpeeling the layers not just of one's personal journey of relationships that have been founded in misunderstandings of one's needs, but the historical and inherited designs of relationships, we see that we may have made decisions about what relationships are by watching our grandparents and parents. She gently lets the reader understand that dysfunctional or unwise relationship choices may have come from our background as well as our own actions. This book is a great addition to the study that any person in recovery could read to help them dig a little deeper into, what for many of us in substance recovery, is a co-occurring disorder. The exercises and affirmations are a great way to do some personal investigation at an emotional level, while the intellectual part of you absorbs the words.

Add this book to your library and read it! You will discover more about your self- damaging and self-denying patterns and learn that ". . . it's time to put the focus on you and not the object of your obsession."

Kyczy Hawk

Yoga teacher who specializes in teaching yoga in treatment centers and jails, and is herself in long-term recovery Author of *Yogic Tools for Recovery; Yoga and the Twelve-Step Path*

LOVE
SMACKED

How to Stop the Cycle of Relationship Addiction and
Codependency to Find Everlasting Love

Sherry Gaba, LCSW
Beth Adelman

AUTHORS PLACE
— P R E S S —

Published by Authors Place Press
9885 Wyecliff Drive, Suite 200
Highlands Ranch, CO 80126
Authorsplace.com

ISBN: 978-1-62865-740-1

CONTENTS

INTRODUCTION 1

CHAPTER 1
What Is Relationship Addiction? 21

CHAPTER 2
Obsession and Abandonment 39

CHAPTER 3
The Codependency Dance. 59

CHAPTER 4
Settling for Less 70

CHAPTER 5
Breaking up Is Hard to Do 87

CHAPTER 6
Letting Go of Your Inner Child 95

CHAPTER 7
Something to Believe In. 109

CHAPTER 8
You Don't Complete Me:
Learning to Live Fabulously on Your Own 120

CHAPTER 9
Dating Without Desperation. 138

CHAPTER 10
Creating Authentic Partnerships and Everlasting Love 150

APPENDIX 159

INTRODUCTION

SHERRY'S STORY

There I was, a year after my father had passed away, four years since my fourth divorce, two years after my dog, Max, died, and it was as if I had just woken up from a very long nightmare. My father's death had put me in a depression and down a rabbit hole that went way beyond losing him. I had been beating myself up for all the relationships that had failed, feeling sorry for myself that I had to grieve alone. How unfair, I thought, that my dad died and I had no shoulder to cry on.

Suddenly waking up from what seemed like a very bad dream, I no longer felt numb, disconnected, medicated, or asleep. I no longer felt the need to destroy my self-esteem with endless shame attacks because I had been so "unlucky in love." I had spent a year grieving my first love, my father, and I was ready to feel again—to feel connected, to belong to something greater than myself. I could only describe this process as a spiritual awakening. My father was gone, but I was alive and he was channeling through me the way to claw out of this hole I was in.

There still wasn't a day that I didn't miss my beloved dad, but I knew he wanted me to stop punishing myself and forgive myself for my mistakes—which I was viewing as transgressions. I needed to let my dad go to his final resting place, and to find deep compassion for myself for all my relationships that I had seen as failures. Instead, I decided, they were stepping stones toward something I didn't know quite yet. These intimate relationships needed to be reframed with a new perspective. Maybe there were lessons here that I needed to learn. And perhaps they needed to be shared with the world. Perhaps my history could make a difference in someone else's life.

The social worker in me would like nothing more than to help someone else go through a different sliding door that might change their lives forever. Perhaps the pain I endured had a purpose; it was time to move from the final stages of grieving and tell my story. But what was this story I needed to tell? I knew I had to share something about my past, but what? Was it my history of codependent relationships? Was it my history of multiple divorces? Was it my history of a "poor picker" when it came to choosing husbands? Was it love addiction? Or was it the trials of being a single mother?

Yes, I had to admit all those things were true, but I realized my story was much bigger. I had never heard of it before, but it was as real as my dad being gone was real: I was a romance and relationship addict. I was using falling in love and getting married as a way to numb myself. This was a huge epiphany for me. What was pulling at me was an illness I never even knew I had. You wouldn't find it in the Diagnostic and Statistical Manual of Mental Disorders. No, this was something different, and I needed to dig deeper.

My story begins sixty years ago in a suburb of the San Fernando Valley known as Van Nuys. Those were the days when there were no freeways and a trip to the maternity ward was more of a challenge. My mother's water broke at six a.m. on February 21, 1959, waking her up. It was quite scary for my mom, I learned later, because not only was this unexpected and way too early, but she had given birth to a stillborn baby five and a half months into her pregnancy a year before. That was her first birth, and she never even knew if it was a boy or a girl. The hospital staff didn't tell you in those days when you had a miscarriage; they never let you see the baby and properly grieve. Miscarriages were hidden away like some horrible disease that needed to be forgotten.

Although I can't explain how, I know—or at least in my heart I believe—my mom lost a baby girl. I have always felt deep in my core that I lost a sister. Years later, a medium told me my mother lost a baby girl before I was born and that the soul of that baby was reborn in my daughter. Whether I choose to accept that literally or metaphorically, it's quite beautiful. My parents always told me my daughter felt more like a daughter to them than a first grandchild.

My mother and father were scared silly they would lose another baby the night my mother's water broke. They rushed to the hospital in Encino, and my mother gave birth to me at 6:59 a.m. I lay helpless in an incubator, brought into this world two and half months early. My parents were told I was what the hospital staff called a fifty-fifty baby: I had a 50 percent chance of living or dying. I was only three pounds, two ounces.

In those days, premature babies were not given the extra attention they receive today. Hospitals didn't have specialists to teach new parents the skills they needed to love, nurture, and bond with a preemie. They didn't understand the vital early importance of touch. Instead, I lay there, helpless and alone in a tiny incubator, oxygen over my nose so I could breathe and feeding tubes in my little feet so I could be nourished. I did not experience the love I so desperately needed from my mother because I was whisked away from her immediately. There was no contact with my mother, except her watching me from a maternity ward window. The hospital staff thought I would be in danger from germs if anyone on the outside, including my own mother, held me. Only the hospital nurses and doctors were allowed to touch, hold, and care for me.

I lay there in that incubator alone and afraid, not knowing to whom I belonged. Although I don't remember the experience mentally, studies have shown we have something called cell memory, so whatever we have forgotten in our minds, our bodies can still remember. This set me up for my first experience with abandonment and my first major trauma, and it laid the foundation for severe separation anxiety and abandonment issues in all my later intimate relationships.

I am convinced this also set me up for severe generalized anxiety disorder and depression. From the time I can remember, long into my adult years, I suffered from profound separation anxiety when I thought my parents were leaving me—which happened a lot in my early developmental years. My mother went back to work nights almost immediately, leaving me with my dad to care for me. I always felt more bonded with my dad, and as I look back, I can now understand why.

I was treated for anxiety and depression in my thirties, but that was only a Band-Aid to help soothe the ache of my early abandonment and separation. It was not until my late forties that I discovered trauma work with an experienced trauma specialist; it opened up a whole new world for me. This was the beginning of the process of waking up from a life of disassociation and emptiness that I could only describe as a very powerful black hole. Suddenly, rather than feeling disassociated from my body and feelings, I could be grounded and in the moment without being terrified.

After a few years of a type of therapy called somatic experiencing (a process that guides a person to slowly complete and resolve their physical and emotional responses to trauma), it dawned on me that I was set up a very long time ago to make the poor choices I made in all my relationships—including four failed marriages. I chose what I had always known: partners who were distant and unavailable because, after all, I was unavailable to myself. I could never feel comfortable alone, and I could never feel comfortable in a relationship. What an awakening it was to learn that all the terror of abandonment I felt in intimate relationships was part of a pattern created on that fateful morning in 1959.

My first experience with what I will call relationship addiction began at age twelve. However, even before that, I would feel jealous if my childhood friend decided to play with someone else, or if I was the one not invited to a sleepover. That's a normal kid reaction—up to a point—but my jealousy was extreme. I would cry nonstop if my parents went out on a Saturday night. My brother would wave goodbye to them, thrilled to be left with a babysitter, while I screamed for them not to leave me.

This feeling of emptiness whenever I was alone continued throughout my life. The only way to ease that excruciating pain I felt—physically in my body—was to fill it up with anything: food, love, drugs, alcohol, shopping, working, or anything I believed could fill the void at that moment.

My twelve-year-old crush was a boy who lived directly across the street from me. I met him while hanging out at a neighbor's house. I was sure this was love at first sight. He had the brightest blue eyes I had ever seen. We made eye contact, and it must have felt as if I was bonding for the very first time. We danced to the song "Sugar Sugar" in my friend's backyard, and I was in love. I spent the next two years obsessing and fantasizing about him until one night when he was babysitting and my brother went off to bed, we sat on the couch and I had my very first kiss.

In the summer of 1973, when I was fourteen, he asked me out on our first date. We went to a famous steak house in Westwood Village. The Rolling Stones song "Angie" was playing on the radio as we drove from Beverly Canyon in his yellow Mustang. I was by far the happiest teenager that summer night.

The next three years I spent up in his bedroom surrounded by Escher posters, smoking a lot of pot, snorting a lot of cocaine, and swallowing a lot of Quaaludes until I graduated high school at age seventeen in 1976. During my last year of high school, I decided I really needed to have other experiences with boys, because after all, I had spent all of high school locked up in my first love's bedroom, numb from love and drugs. I begged my parents to let me go away to college because I had it all figured out: I was going to go to school in San Diego, meet and have lots of experiences with different boys to get that out of my system, and when I was done, my first love would be waiting for me, and we would live happily ever after.

I went to college, did a lot of drinking, and messed around a lot that freshman year at San Diego State University, but my first love was not waiting for me when I came home. In fact, he no longer lived across the street; he had moved to UC Santa Cruz and immediately met someone. I was shocked he didn't wait for me and couldn't believe he could end something I had so perfectly planned out for us. He had thrown away our future marriage and children. What was he thinking?

The question—which I did not ask—was: What was *I* thinking? The truth is, I wasn't thinking. There wasn't a logical brain cell in my body. I had the same panic, fear, and crippling pain anyone might feel at lost love. However, there was something more to it—a kind of hysteria, a lack of self-reflection, and a complete lack of logic. I was in withdrawal, like any addict.

Instead of grieving this loss, I, of course, went searching for my next hostage as a way to avoid the emptiness I could hardly bear to feel. I spent the next couple of years trying to fill up my aching heart by dating and disco dancing. It was the late 1970s and early 1980s—the era of punk rock, John Travolta, and *Saturday Night Fever*. I spent weekends either on a date or on the dance floor dancing to Donna Summer, the Bee Gees, and the Village People.

I was not out for fun, though; this was serious business. I was on the hunt for Mr. Right. I disco danced my way into the arms of my first husband and the father of my only daughter. We both wore red pants when we first met, and to me, that seemed to make us the perfect match. My girlfriends laughed all the way home when he said he would call but didn't even write down my phone number. He boldly said he would memorize it forever, and I took him seriously. Always seeking external validation, I thought to myself, "This guy must really like me. I must be amazing."

We were married two years after we met, with several break-ups in between. That should have been a warning to me, but of course, it wasn't.

I was only twenty-two—the very first one of my friends to get married. Most of my friends were just finishing up college and starting careers. But being afraid no one would ever want me again, I didn't simply go out with the first person who took me seriously—I married him.

I had already dropped out of college to become a makeup artist, so with no degree and no real living situation, I moved right out of my parents' home into my very first apartment with my new husband. I went from being financially supported by my parents to being financially supported by my husband. I had never lived alone.

I got pregnant a year later, and a year after that my husband left my daughter and me and moved to New York. My worst fear was realized—and I was alone with my one-year-old daughter. At least by then I had gone back to college and earned a bachelor's degree in journalism, although I don't remember that degree making me feel optimistic. All I can remember is that I felt abandoned, helpless, and as alone as I had twenty-six years earlier in that incubator. The pattern of being abandoned was playing out again.

Had early abandonment set me up for more abandonment? Was I creating this reality for myself? At the time, I didn't see the link, but now I think the Law of Attraction was at work in my life. The Law of Attraction states that we create our own reality—both positive and negative—by the thoughts and actions we put out into the universe. I lived in constant terror of being abandoned. That's all I thought about—and that's what I got.

I begged my parents to allow me to move in with them. All I was thinking about was getting married again, and how was I going to attract another man with a child upstairs crying? The last thing I signed up for was to be a young single mother. Luckily, my parents refused to allow me to move in. I know that sounds harsh, and at the time I thought it was, but today I know that would have been enabling behavior—enabling me to continue being dependent on others and never taking responsibility for my own life.

I dated frantically to fill the inevitable emptiness that engulfed me, and by the time my daughter was five years old, I was on to marriage number two—to a man I had known for just six weeks. This time I was convinced it was love at first sight—again. I met him at a friend's party; he was gorgeous and had a New York accent. I was always very attracted to men from New York, probably because my first love, my father, was from Brooklyn. Husband number two was more unavailable than husband number one had been. He was a workaholic attempting to live the Hollywood producer dream, and after ten months he too walked out on me.

I was again left to raise my daughter on my own. Only this time, my daughter was old enough to feel abandoned as well. Although I am convinced she has some memory of the trauma of her biological dad leaving when she was one, those memories are physical rather than psychological.

Looking back now, what did I expect? I didn't know the person I married. I had made up a fantasy about a man from New York who looked good and smelled good. Was he anything like that man I created in my head? I didn't even know.

I worked hard in sales and continued to raise my daughter, and two months after husband number two left, I jumped into another relationship with a New Yorker—this time, one transplanted from England. He completely charmed me off my feet with his devilish English accent, and even better, he was six years younger than me. Talk about external validation!

We spent the next year traveling back and forth between New York and Los Angeles. Our long-distance love was the hottest and most romantic relationship I had ever experienced. He sent me love letters, we had long talks on the phone, and I kept telling myself eventually he would not be able to live without me and would move to LA.

As time passed, though, I found it harder and harder to deny the reality of our situation. I knew he was never going to move, and I could not uproot my daughter and move away from my parents. We were doomed from the beginning; the intensity of our relationship had always been a fantasy. It's a lot easier to delude yourself about someone when they live three thousand miles away. We never developed any true intimacy, and he pulled away. Again, the Law of Attraction was recreating my early abandonment.

When that relationship ended, I joined Great Expectations, which was the 1990s version of Internet dating. It was a dating service where you sat for hours looking at videos of people to date who might fit your criteria. This was a relationship addict's dream, because if one date didn't go well, there was always another video to watch and another man to date.

It never occurred to me to just sit still and learn to live my life on my own, making a little family of just my daughter and me. No, I had to be married—and married to a modern version of Prince Charming.

I met my third husband through the video dating service. On the outside, he looked like he had everything I was looking for. He came from a big Jewish family who attended temple regularly. He seemed close to his brothers, who had amazing wives. My own relationship with my brother and his wife had its ups and downs, so I was eager to have a real family and fill in what I felt was lacking in mine. At the time, he could give that to me, so I was sure he was the right fit. He seemed to have the life I wanted, and I was in a hurry to get it. I didn't look any deeper. Like any addict, I focused on what feels good or looks good on the outside, rather than understanding that happiness comes from the inside.

What I didn't see (or chose not to see) was his verbally abusive temper, his sexual deviations, and his obsessive-compulsive disorder that left me crying night after night. I was never able to please him or meet his neurotic and uncontrollable needs. For example, if I didn't clean the bathtub after using it, wiping out every last drop of water, he would start screaming. He was even compulsive about my daughter's eating habits—which, frankly, were none of his damn business.

We dated for two years, and I felt driven to please him. I was going to get the approval and acceptance I missed from my own parents through him. You may see women in damaging, dangerous relationships and wonder why they don't just walk away. This is one of the reasons. I was also thirty-six years old and panicked about missing my chance to have more children; my biological clock was ticking away. The thought of being alone—again—was more terrifying to me than anything he could say or do.

Two weeks before the wedding I thought about calling it off, but with three hundred guests about to attend the "wedding of the century," I didn't have the courage to cancel it. I took a tranquilizer and unhappily married a man I knew, even then, was not "Mr. Right." I should have known when a pedestal of flowers fell on my wedding dress before I even walked down the aisle that this was my biggest mistake ever.

My new husband spent our married life together criticizing my parenting abilities, obsessing about my weight (even though I had no weight issues), and controlling me nonstop. When his abuse started to affect my daughter's well-being, I had no choice but to leave. After four months of matrimony, I took two plastic garbage bags, packed up as much as I could, and was out of there with my daughter.

As I look back, I'm proud I left but sad I couldn't leave him before the wedding. He was as abusive before we were married as after. My insecurity and neediness took over, and I had made another bad choice—not only for me but for my daughter.

Like the relationship addict I was, I immediately renewed my search for my next great love by placing an ad in the *Los Angeles Times*. I met a single dad of three small boys, ages two, five, and seven. At least I was making better choices by seeking a relationship with someone who might understand how tough it is to be a single parent. My third husband had hounded me constantly about how I was parenting my daughter. I wanted to meet someone who was so busy raising his own children that he would not feel the need to control me and my parenting.

My new boyfriend had a great sense of humor and was extremely successful. He owned his own business and his own home; he was very responsible, and I was attracted to that. I was crazy about him and his three sons. Eventually, my daughter and I moved in with them.

Unfortunately, with all that responsibility came his obsession with work and his laptop. I spent the next six years chasing him, begging for the attention I so craved. He was a workaholic, busy raising three kids, and was still obsessed with his ex-wife. This man could not give me what I needed. Although he was a great provider, he didn't know how to be emotionally available. He would show me he loved me by fixing my car or helping me on my computer, rather than buying me flowers and jewelry—the things I associated with love.

At the time, I blamed everything on him, but now I understand that maybe some of our disconnect was my fault. My insatiable appetite for attention was a tall order no one would ever be able to fill. In all my intimate relationships, I continued to feel alone and disconnected.

We were engaged on and off, and every time we got close to planning a future, both of us would find some way to fight, break up, and sabotage things. I think in the end, we both feared true intimacy and did what we could to undermine any future together. After six years of this, I did the final breaking up and was heartbroken. I knew he was never going to marry me so I moved out of his house. Again, I was recreating the patterns of my past.

During my brief third marriage, I had enrolled in graduate school at the University of Southern California to become a social worker. I stuck with it through a handful of break-ups, three moves, and finally, graduation. After I graduated, I landed an internship and then a job. I continued to raise my daughter as a single mother, since her dad was living on the East Coast.

Before I go on, I must make it clear that although my traumatic birth experience profoundly affected my future intimate relationships, this same trauma has given me the resilience to endure tremendous pain—and especially multiple losses in the past nine years. I had great determination to survive from the moment I took my first breath. Sometimes the energy from early trauma puts you in a position to be a survivor. If that energy is harnessed correctly, you can accomplish great things. I think becoming a social worker was one of those great accomplishments for me. I graduated from school with a master's degree in social work—the first one in my family to finish a four-year college degree and to go to graduate school. At age forty-two, I finally took the exams and became a licensed clinical social worker.

He had just gotten out of rehab and had been drinking since his early twenties. He was gorgeous, with green eyes, a great build, a native New Yorker, charming, and he smelled great. I was smitten. He had no job and was sleeping on a futon at his sister's place after a five-year run of addiction and alcoholism. With his newfound sobriety, he was in no position to be in a relationship. With my relationship problems, neither was I. But, like the addicts we both were, we just plunged ahead without thinking about the consequences. As I studied for my social work degree, I had learned about codependent relationships, where one person supports or enables another person's dysfunctional behavior. I learned that codependency always goes both ways: both people are enablers; both people are enabled. But I still couldn't see how codependent I was.

I did not have any idea what I was getting into with this man or where his addiction could take him. Recovery from addiction and alcoholism really is a one day at a time for the rest of your life. I just assumed if he was sober, he would be sober forever. Once again, I surfed the elation I felt in the moment without bothering to look up at the wave that was eventually going to crash over me.

For the next two years, we were together and I watched from the sidelines as he rebuilt his life. Eventually we were married, and he moved into my home with me and my dog, Max. My daughter, now in her third year of college, had just moved out. I was needy and afraid to live alone, so it was no accident that husband number four was moving in as my daughter was moving out.

The first five years of our marriage felt like a long honeymoon. We traveled, enjoyed our families, and were really happy. I wrote a book and was a therapist on VH1's *Celebrity Rehab,* and my husband was my biggest fan. I felt loved and supported; I was comfortable and content. Unfortunately, in year five he had a serious accident at work. He ended up taking prescription painkillers, and that eventually led to his drinking again. I put my husband into a handful of rehab programs, but he couldn't stay clean. He lied to me about it again and again, and I so wanted to believe his lies, but eventually I couldn't. After his last relapse, I threatened to divorce him if he refused to seriously enter a 12-step program and get a sponsor. I had finally learned something about relationship addiction and was actually ready to set boundaries for myself.

Then I got a call from him at two a.m. He was drunk and forgot where he parked his car. I told him never to come home again, and I divorced him. I am the one who ended it, but I still felt abandoned. He'd chosen his alcoholism over me, and, like the addict I also was, I had a hard time letting go. Even after we divorced, I continued to be his friend and tried to help him get sober. I knew in trying to save him I was losing myself, but I did it anyway. That was when I started to attend Al-Anon meetings—a program for family and friends of alcoholics.

It wasn't until my third year of the program that I realized I had long ago lost myself in my ex-husband's drama. I developed shingles and a host of other health issues from the stress, and in my own relationship addiction I thought I could save him from himself so he could be with me. What I didn't understand was that I couldn't want his sobriety more than he did. I knew he had his own higher power and I had mine, but I didn't stop trying to change him. There is no question that I enabled him and was definitely addicted to my relationship with him. Today, I have detached with love and understand he has his own path and I have mine.

Since joining the Al-Anon program, I have developed lifelong friendships, taken up canoeing, and for the first time ever, I know in my deepest core I can live a good life with or without a man. I do not need another person to fill me up.

Four and a half years ago I lost my dad, and I grieved for my very first love. I watched my mother abuse alcohol as she grieved for sixty years of not knowing any life other than with my father. She stepped into her own codependent relationship with a new boyfriend very soon after my father died—reminding me that addiction is often passed down through generations. My grandmother, a compulsive gambler, was married four times. Her last husband stole everything from her apartment as she lay dying of cancer in the hospital.

I don't know how the rest of my journey will play out, but I do know I have a level of self-love that I never had before. I also know relationship addiction can be handed down, and as I participate in my new granddaughter's life, I hope I can set an example for her and make sure she knows that she is perfectly whole with or without an intimate relationship; love will find her without her having to addictively seek it. I have had the opportunity to observe from afar the mothering, attachment, and bonding that is taking place between my daughter, a new mother, and her own daughter. I know how crucial this experience will be in determining my granddaughter's future relationships. Because she has gotten what she needs emotionally in the first few years of life and beyond, I have a lot of hope that relationship addiction will not be a problem for this little girl.

My hope, now that I have discovered my own story, is to share this syndrome of romance and relationship addiction with the world. I am no longer a victim of multiple marriages, but a victor, ready to share what I've learned with the thousands, maybe millions, of individuals out there—the majority of them women—who, as I did, use relationships as an avoidance strategy. I hope my own story will motivate others to think twice before walking down the aisle and buying into that false belief that happily ever after is the only goal. Lost love can be transformed into something much greater.

Relationship addiction is as real as any addiction. It goes beyond love addiction, tapping into the fantasies that popular culture bombards us with—that we all have a perfect soul mate waiting for us who will fix everything in our lives. Those are fantasies I once believed too.

My job now is to share what I have learned from the multiple relationships I entered into and out of. I have discovered the pattern that wove through them, and I am here to share that pattern with you. I've learned that being in a relationship is not the only way to avoid the excruciating emptiness that we all have experienced in our lives at one time or another. There are much healthier ways to fill that void. When you learn them, any relationship you do get into will be more grounded and realistic, and will have a better chance of bringing you real happiness.

BETH'S STORY

My story is quite different from Sherry's, and I count myself very lucky indeed to have found the love of my life in my second marriage. While working with Sherry on this book, I had some important insights into why my first marriage failed and why my second one is so solid. For me, as well, it goes back to my family, and especially my father.

My parents placed a high value on independence. They wanted me to be able to care for myself, but it went beyond that; they wanted me to be totally self-sufficient and self-contained. Although very early on my mother would be there if I asked for help, by the time I started school she began turning down those requests, explaining that I had to learn how to take care of myself. No hug if I got hurt as a kid, no help navigating difficult relationships as a teenager, and no help paying for things as a young adult. My father would get annoyed if I asked for anything—especially anything that required an effort from him. His basic message was that asking reflected my intolerable selfishness.

I remember one year I was returning to college after the summer, and had to catch a train to Chicago. I had a huge, heavy suitcase that I could barely push, much less lift. The day before, I asked my father if he could drive me to the train station. He replied that he'd pay for a taxi. I told him I really could not manage my suitcase and needed help in the station as well. He shouted, "You've got some nerve asking me. You should have thought of that before you decided to pack all those things." He never did take me to the train station.

There were times when my father could be very fun and loving, but the lesson I learned from him was that love comes only on others' terms and when I don't ask for what I need. When I got married, it was to a man who absolutely agreed. And since I was crazy in love with him and needed him to love me, I did whatever he wanted and didn't say much about what I wanted. Occasionally, when I did, he either accused me of being selfish or just ignored my request.

The more I tried to give him what he wanted, the less he seemed interested in anything I might want. I had expected the opposite: that the more I tried to make him happy and the less I asked for myself, the more he'd try to make me happy. About three years into my marriage, I knew that deep down I was angry and unhappy, but I thought that's what love looked like. It took another six years before I finally insisted that my husband leave.

What changed? We went to couples counseling (my idea) for about six months. At one of the later sessions, I asked him point blank, "I told you many times in therapy exactly what I need from you and you have never done any of it. Why not?"

He answered, "Because those things are important to you, not to me." I actually gasped. It was a gasp of epiphany. In a real partnership based on true love, the things that are important to your partner are important to you. I had made that so for myself, embracing his social circle and the things he loved, sending money to his family, living the lifestyle he preferred, and being as self-contained as my father had wanted me to be—always hoping that would inspire my husband to reciprocate. Suddenly I knew I was never, ever going to get what I needed from this man. I would never be happy with him. I had to stop kidding myself.

I remember telling my grandmother about our split. I know she meant well, but she said something that I think was very characteristic of her generation: "He's not such a bad guy, he has a good job, and you are thirty-six years old. You know it's extremely unlikely you'll ever find anyone else."

I replied, "I would rather be alone for the rest of my life, with at least the possibility that I might one day be happy, than stay with this man and know for sure that I will never be happy." When I said it, I felt brave but not necessarily 100 percent sure. I felt a bit closer to being sure when, just a few months after my husband moved out, everyone I knew told me how much younger I looked!

Of course, it was still very difficult to be single again at age thirty-six. I'd been married for nine years, during which time I had come to believe I deserved nothing at all in a relationship. My self-esteem had taken a hard hit, and I never felt comfortable asking for anything.

Then a cousin who had divorced and happily remarried called me up and gave me a piece of advice that changed my life: "I watched you stay in a marriage for a very long time that seemed, even from the outside, to be abusive. You have to figure out why you stayed so long and put up with so much. Because if you don't figure it out, you're going to keep doing the same thing again and again."

A friend introduced me to his therapist, who told me something that opened my eyes: "People marry others who share their world view. If you have a world view that doesn't actually work for you, you are going to marry someone who ultimately can't give you what you need."

Changing your world view is not an easy thing. I had a great therapist, though, and we worked hard together to understand how my parents' conditional love had created a world view for me in which my needs had to be completely negated. At heart, I'm a 1950s kind of woman in that I like to "take care of my man," but I learned a man deserves that only if he also takes care of me. I came to understand how special I am and how much I deserve.

I reconnected with a lot of friends and also made friends with other single women in their thirties. We were all in the same boat, but rather than complain about it, we just shared a lot of laughs. I felt more and more sure that the bold statement I had made to my grandmother was really true.

I went on plenty of dates, but I was just looking for fun guys. I enjoyed dating and being reminded that I was actually attractive and nice to be with. In fact, the guys I dated told me they liked my company partly because I seemed so confident—not at all fixated on relationships. Ironically, the fact that I didn't care if I ever got married again is what set me up for solid relationships.

Now the independence I had cultivated all my life was paired with the knowledge that I deserved to get what I wanted. I was in a few relationships but ended them when the man failed to reciprocate my generosity of spirit. I deserved a man who wanted to take care of me the way I wanted to take care of him, one who would put me at the center of his life the way I was willing to put him at the center of mine. And if I never found him, I could have a great time dating and hanging out with my girlfriends.

When I met Craig, I still felt that way. He was handsome, funny, and really smart. We liked a lot of the same things. I didn't think about anything more than that. Slowly, though, I began to see how much he was willing to give—even when I didn't ask. As things got serious between us, I started asking for what I needed, and to my delight, when I told him, he gave it to me. If I told him he had hurt me, he was truly sorry and changed his ways. One day, he confessed to me that I was already at the center of his life, and he would do whatever it took to make sure I stayed there. I believed him—because he had already shown me it was true. Twenty-two years later, it still is.

Whatever your path, whatever inspired you to pick up this book, we both hope it helps you view your own story with clarity and insight, so you can change your world view and get the relationship you deserve— or not. All that really matters is that you feel comfortable and worthy in your own skin. You are the same deserving person, whether you are with a partner or without one. When you can live that truth, everything changes.

In this book, you'll find that we ask you a lot of tough questions. If it seems like we're challenging you, we are. We're asking you to examine and rethink many of your core beliefs, and this is certainly a challenge!

These questions are not rhetorical. You should answer them—all of them. If you need to put the book down and think about a question for a while, do it. We'll still be here when you get back.

You're alone as you read this book, so your answers will be private. In a way, that makes them even tougher: You'll know if you told the truth, and you'll know if you skipped the really hard questions.

This questioning process will help you get to the roots of your addiction and, ultimately, will help you leave it behind. So be fearless and be strong with yourself—it's the only way to set yourself free. But be kind and nurturing too. You deserve it.

CHAPTER 1

WHAT IS RELATIONSHIP ADDICTION?

We are biologically hardwired to connect with other people and go through life two by two, and culturally hardwired to be in formal relationships. In Western cultures, more than 90 percent of people marry by age fifty.

For some people, this hardwiring goes haywire, and they see life as a choice between living in a kind of fantasy romance novel or the sheer hell (for them) of being unattached. In healthy relationships, after the initial attraction where couples idealize and attach to each other, love matures and changes. For example, it becomes less intense but more secure. However, people with relationship addiction never get past the initial stages of falling in love. They are obsessed with the idea of being in a romantic relationship, no matter the cost. They become dependent on the object of their affection, hoping somehow this person will complete their life and create a kind of happily ever after. Their expectations are unrealistic, so inevitably they are disappointed. Their relationships are ultimately never truly satisfying, yet they can't seem to live without them.

Relationships pile up, becoming increasingly tangled and messy. Romances become serial disasters because they jump in again and again without first doing the work of unearthing the trauma and issues that keep them in their cycle of addiction. A break-up—even a really tough one—can be a chance to learn from the past and build something new. However, people need sufficient time to recover and get their priorities straight before entering into new relationships. If they don't take this time to heal, they tend to repeat their mistakes.

Relationship addicts are so in love with love that they continually move from one romance to another, always on the rebound, never giving themselves time to heal and learn how to be independent. They hook up again and again just to avoid feeling lonely—or worse, to avoid feeling "abnormal." But there are things that happen to us in love-addicted relationships that, if we don't learn from them and don't realize why we are picking who we are picking, we will keep repeating. That's something I (Sherry) tell my clients all the time. Addiction is something you keep doing over and over again, somehow expecting different results.

We know addiction is a disease, but it's also a behavior. It's a way people behave. The problem is, it's a behavior people can't stop themselves from doing, even when they are hurting themselves. Sometimes they don't realize that they are damaging themselves, or that the pain will inevitably come. But even when they know they are hurting themselves, even when they know what's coming, they can't stop.

It's common to think of addiction as related to some physical substance—smoking, drinking, or taking drugs, for example. Psychologists call these substance addictions. But we now know that people can also become addicted to mood-altering activities and behaviors, which can cause the same euphoric states as mood-altering substances. These are called process or lifestyle addictions, and include things like gambling, binge eating, sex, the Internet, and shopping.

HOW DOES THE RELATIONSHIP ADDICTION PROCESS UNFOLD?

The key to distinguishing relationship addiction from the normal ups and downs of dating and relationships is to examine the frequency or severity of those ups and downs. If a person has five happy relationships and one unhappy one, they are not likely a relationship addict. If they are unhappy in every relationship, and yet feel even worse on their own, likely they're addicted to romance, love, and relationships.

Relationship addiction is painful; sufferers find it excruciating to be alone. The relationship takes over their waking mind and uses up their emotional energy, as they keep reinventing themselves to make sure the object of their obsession will continue to choose them.

An addictive relationship begins with a typical attraction to someone, but it morphs into idealizing that person, even if the relationship junkie doesn't know them very well. The addict is so desperate to hook up with someone that they become blinded by the fantasy of love at first sight and obsessively preoccupied with their love interest. Everything else in their life gets shoved aside, and they spend endless hours daydreaming and obsessing about where this relationship will go and what fantasy it might fulfill.

People who are not relationship junkies know one person can't possibly fulfill all their needs. They include friends and family in their lives and are comfortable having no relationship at all if the right person doesn't come along. Relationship addicts, though, are looking for just one person to fill an insatiable emptiness in their lives. They believe this new love is the answer to all their unmet hopes and dreams. Being alone feels intolerable, so this person, this relationship, will forever save them from loneliness and rejection.

The relationship junkie invests everything in each new relationship, often right from the start. They become completely dependent on it and begin to fear rejection, disappointment, or betrayal. If the relationship ends, all their hopes and dreams will be obliterated. This sets the stage for obsession.

Obsessive love is a sort of desperate longing. It never feels whole, never feels nurturing, and never feels safe. During the obsessive stage, the addict tries to control the object of their love, insisting that they meet their needs at any cost. They want more time, more attention, more consideration. They want their partner to be able to read their mind and fulfill their fantasies. If they get any hint of rejection, they go into panic; this could be something as innocent as their partner saying they don't feel like meeting up tonight or are tired and want to go to bed early. The addict's brain starts taking something simple and turns it into something complicated. Their nervous system goes into overdrive, and they try to avoid feeling the pain of what they see as rejection by searching for anything to replace it.

This is when many relationships begin to spiral downward. The partner begins to pull back because the relationship feels smothering, overbearing, all-consuming. They may avoid the relationship addict, or they may be more direct and just say, "You're smothering me!" This disengagement triggers the addict's attachment issues and core fear of abandonment. In an addicted relationship, though, this spiraling downward doesn't necessarily mean the end of the relationship—at least not for the addict. The addict has become completely dependent on this relationship and will go to great lengths to deny and avoid the truth that the relationship is in trouble.

The stress of endless denial, endless stories and lies they tell themselves, and endless anxiety takes a toll, often leading to substance addictions such as food, alcohol, or drugs. I (Sherry) identify not as an alcoholic, but as someone who is a relationship addict, which at times led to me abusing substances when the relationships failed to meet my needs or eventually ended. I also used substances when I was dating as a way to self-medicate my anxieties about the inevitable uncertainties of any new relationship. The periods of not knowing if a date might lead to a serious relationship was incredibly anxiety-producing for me. It was those up-in-the-air periods that made me feel the most uncomfortable in my skin. Sometimes, the only solution was to self-medicate. I never became an alcoholic but I certainly abused alcohol during those periods of unease.

THE CYCLE OF ADDICTION

The cycle of relationship addiction has several stages, which are laid out quite elegantly in Pia Mellody's book, *Facing Love Addiction.* These stages begin with the relationship addict being attracted to a partner who is unavailable in some way. This kind of person recreates their early childhood wounds of being with caregivers who either abandoned or neglected them. They need someone to take care of them in a way their early caregivers did not, but, paradoxically, they typically pick someone who is like their early caregivers and can't actually fulfill that need.

When the relationship addict starts to feel good about being wanted and adored, their childhood fantasy of being rescued kicks in. They feel relieved that they won't ever have to be alone and believe this fantasy person will make them feel whole. There is a strong desire to merge identities, so the partner can banish their deep fear of abandonment. However, the addict is not truly seeing who this partner is; instead, they are responding to a delusion of what they want their partner to be. There is a kind of emotional and even physical high, similar to how a substance abuser might feel about their drug of choice.

By this time, the addict begins to get needier and needier, which often causes their love interest to pull away. The addict is still in denial about who this partner really is, but eventually, when the denial starts to wear off, the addict begins to re-experience their early childhood wounds. Desperation kicks in. The partner is now becoming more and more unavailable, and the addict responds by trying to control everything and everyone in the relationship.

The addict experiences the most excruciating pain during the next phase, withdrawal. This phase is characterized by pain, fear, rage, jealousy, emptiness, frustration, or a combination of any and all these emotions. The relationship addict turns their anger and disappointment in on themselves, and this can result in depression, suicide, anxiety, rage, and obsession. Controlling behaviors increase, such as nonstop texting, driving by their partner's home or workplace, and other desperate means to make connections with their love object. The relationship becomes more and more toxic and manipulative as the addict desperately tries to gain control. Obsession, in fact, is an attempt to self-medicate the excruciating pain of withdrawal.

The experience of withdrawal feels like something is missing from one's very core, especially when it is part of a break-up. The addict is longing for the attachment they have lost. Obsessive thoughts get out of control, and the debilitating pain is as severe as any drug user craving a fix. Because the stage of withdrawal is one of the most painful, we will spend more time looking at it in chapter 5.

A client Sherry was seeing in therapy told her, "I couldn't deal with the emotional pain I was experiencing. I felt either high or low at any given moment, and I was full of angst. I felt obsessive, depressed, and a deep emptiness. It was as if someone was stepping on my chest. I was crying all the time, couldn't sleep, and felt like I was going to die. I didn't think I would ever find someone to love me again, and I didn't think I could live without him."

The emptiness of withdrawal, the obsession, anger, betrayal, and resentment penetrate every cell. There is no distraction to ease the incredible pain. It is a stage where the addict feels they will never be loved again; other symptoms may include anxiety, panic, fear, nausea, weight changes, insomnia, rage, despair, and a profound, desperate desire to connect with the object of their addiction.

During withdrawal, the love addict will go to great lengths of scheming to pull their partner back in, and they may use many of the strategies they learned as an abandoned child. They will manipulate and control, may dress provocatively, cheat, enter into affairs both emotionally and sexually, abandon their partner to make them jealous, and/or become abusive. To avoid the pain of withdrawal and keep themselves hooked into unhealthy relationships, addicts may also try to transform themselves. They believe they must be picture perfect to earn love; this comes from deep feelings of unworthiness, shame, un-lovability, and fear of being left behind. Addicts draw what little self-esteem they have from the sense that they are trying hard and doing the "right thing." The relationship addict believes they are trying to meet their partner's needs, but in fact, everything addicts do, even the things that look the most self-sacrificing, are done to meet their own need to be loved and needed.

They may become overly compliant instead of being authentic and truthful. In fact, relationship addicts are masters of manipulation. They will invest great lengths of time and energy determining what patterns of behavior will produce the desired effects in other people. They may lie, keep secrets, break promises, withhold information, violate boundaries, use sarcasm, or portray themselves as a victim to keep a connection. But because they have tied their identity entirely to their partner, thereby ignoring their own essence, these ploys cause them to feel an intense loss of self and identity—similar to those terrible feelings of being abandoned by the unavailable caregiver. It is as if they are invisible and live in the abyss of nothingness.

All of these tactics are intended to avoid the pain of withdrawal and stem from a host of fears, including fear of emptiness, nothingness, abandonment, loss of control, losing connection, exposure, rejection, insignificance, loss of security, and that self is not enough. It can become so painful that they just can't stand it anymore and will cover it up with denial. They deny the problem, the pain, and the cause. The addict fears any truth that might separate them from the fantasy they have created about their love object. All of these fears prevent the relationship addict from being their authentic self, experiencing self-acceptance, self-love, and self-esteem. Most of their time is spent running from their true self with the mistaken belief that they are keeping themselves safe. The relationship addict gives up their own creativity, spontaneity, authenticity, and value system to avoid the suffering of withdrawal.

Finally, during the last stage of relationship addiction, the addict either leaves the relationship to start this cycle over with a new partner or attempts to get the love object back. Either way, there is no learning from experience, no time or space for healing.

EXERCISE 1. AM I A RELATIONSHIP JUNKIE?

It's time to ask yourself some tough questions. Only you will see the answers to these, so be as honest as you can. Put aside any excuses or rationalizations, and spend some quiet time thinking and reflecting on each statement. The idea here is not to judge yourself, but to start becoming aware of your patterns of behavior. So be honest but not brutal. Be kind to yourself, even if you uncover some uncomfortable realizations.

Respond to these statements using the numbers below. Then add up your total.

2 = I behave this way often.

1 = I sometimes behave this way.

0 = I never behave this way.

1. I am very clingy.
2. I instantly fall in love.
3. When I first meet someone, I obsess about them and where our relationship might go.
4. I fall for anyone who pays attention to me.
5. I overwhelm my partners with attention.
6. I stay in unhealthy relationships.
7. My "picker" seems to be off with potential partners.
8. I trust too easily or trust the wrong people.
9. I feel hopeless after a relationship ends.
10. I feel it's my job to fix my partner.

11.   I have low self-esteem.

12.   I feel lost, especially when I am alone.

13.   I live my life in extremes.

14.   I never feel a part of things.

15.   I can't be alone with myself.

16.   I feel empty without a relationship.

17.   I believe I am going to be alone forever.

18.   I believe I am completely entangled with my partner.

19.   I have trouble saying no to my partner.

20.   I am a chameleon in relationships.

21.   I believe my relationship is my life.

22.   I will stay in a relationship no matter what, even if it's an unhealthy one.

23.   I am afraid my partner will leave me.

24.   Rejection makes me overreact.

25.   I believe my partner can save me.

If your score totaled

3-15 = You are not a relationship junkie, but you tend to make relationships overly important in your life.

16-25 = You are a relationship junkie.

THIS IS YOUR BRAIN ON LOVE

Studies of the brain have found some very interesting parallels between love addiction and substance addiction. Several studies have found that both sexual desire and intense romantic love activate an area of the brain called the nucleus accumbens. When we do things we consider rewarding, this part of the brain (commonly called the pleasure center) releases dopamine and serotonin, two chemicals that give us a surge of pleasure. This pleasure reinforces whatever behavior triggered them; it says, "Yes, what you did just now feels good! Do it again." Romantic love also activates the insula, which is the region of the brain that assigns value to things.

These happen to be the same two parts of the brain that are most affected by addictive drugs. So that initial flush of attraction, the intense romantic love that follows, and the effects of heroin and cocaine all activate the same parts of the brain.

Studies show that losing a lover can, for some, have the same physical and emotional symptoms as withdrawal from a narcotic. For example, a study done at Stony Brook University in New York showed a striking similarity between romantic rejection and cocaine withdrawal cravings. In other words, withdrawal from a significant relationship is a like a drug user craving their drug of choice.

Withdrawal symptoms from drugs, alcohol, or emotional attachment include:

- » Insomnia
- » Disturbed sleep
- » Flu-like symptoms
- » Nausea
- » Vomiting
- » Stomach ailments
- » Dramatic changes in weight
- » Depression
- » Grief states
- » Anxiety
- » Panic
- » Fear
- » Loneliness

- » Obsession
- » Anger
- » Rage
- » Emptiness
- » Denial
- » Despair

These symptoms can require a period of detoxification, so just as drug addicts and alcoholics who want to kick their addiction must abstain from drugs and alcohol, people struggling with process addictions must abstain from their self-destructive behavior. For relationship addicts, that means abstaining from a relationship and, hopefully, entering a program of recovery so the healing process can begin.

DIFFERENT RELATIONSHIPS, DIFFERENT ADDICTS

Relationship junkies are obsessed with being in a relationship, not necessarily with any particular partner, but this can mean different things to different people. Some relationship junkies go from partner to partner—even spouse to spouse—and have no problem letting go of one as long as there is another one to replace them. Then there are relationship addicts who stay with their partner at all costs, even if they are no longer in love, even if they are being abused. Again, they are not addicted to the partner but to the relationship itself.

The third type of relationship junkie is addicted to the idea of romance—not really a relationship or even a person. Romance addicts are addicted to a fantasy partner and a passionate fantasy life, not unlike a Harlequin romance novel. Romance addiction is not about the partner; it's about the romance and all that goes with it, from candlelit dinners to charming getaways to elaborate gifts. The pursuit of romance becomes the addiction, and what they think is love at first sight is really addiction at first sight.

What's common to all these relationships is that even if there is intense infatuation or amazing sex, what the addict is really starving for is an authentic connection—and it's just not there. Authentic connection is based on trust and honesty, but the relationship junkie doesn't feel safe enough to offer either. Although these relationships appear on the outside to be close and connected, the reality is that the relationship junkie doesn't even know the person they are falling in love with. The neurotransmitters oxytocin and dopamine and the profound need to attach to *someone* create an illusion of intimacy.

Relationship addiction isn't about love; it's a frantic search for bonding and belonging, and the relationship often turns into one that is filled with control, fear, and shame. At the bottom of all addictive relationships is an intimacy disorder. Any sort of true intimacy is impossible.

LONGING FOR WHAT WE'VE LOST

Abandonment was at the core of my (Sherry's) addiction—as it is for most relationship addicts. It's an attempt to recover the losses of early childhood. For me, that was my early lack of bonding with my mother. Today, parenting experts call the first sixty minutes after a baby's birth the "golden hour." This is when a mother gets her first opportunity to hold her new baby in her arms. There is something magical that happens during that uninterrupted contact—something that is necessary for the mother-child bond and the growth and development of the child.

I was born premature, so my birth was immediately followed by medical procedures and then I was whisked away to an incubator. Not only did I miss this golden hour, I missed the next three golden months. I spent that time inside a machine in a sterile hospital maternity ward, rather than at home, feeling my mother's touch skin to skin. Today, hospitals know that babies need to be touched and held in order to thrive—physically, as well as emotionally. They even have volunteer "cuddlers" who hold the babies whose parents aren't present. Unfortunately, when I was born, we didn't know how important early touch and holding is for human development.

To make things worse, when I went home three months later, my mother had profound anxiety that something bad would happen to me in her care. When she would attempt to feed me with a bottle, my body was so weak and tiny, I would turn blue in her arms. This was incredibly scary for my mother, and her profound anxiety further damaged the bonding experience. This set me up for an insatiable hunger I believed could only be satisfied by a partner—someone who would hold me forever.

Other people suffering from relationship addiction may have had caregivers who were unavailable physically or emotionally. They may have been neglected or abused as young children—another type of rejection that sets them up for relationship addiction. We know that the greater the intensity of a person's unmet needs, the stronger their addiction to relationships. (We'll look at childhood trauma in more detail in chapter 4.)

The hunger for attachment—stemming from ineffective early bonding or dysfunctional families—are two of the major causes of addictive relationships in adulthood. However, some individuals come from fully functional families that are intact but still become relationship addicts. Often, as adolescents these people never fit in and were rejected or even bullied by their peers. As they enter adolescence, the acceptance of their peers actually becomes more important than the acceptance of their parents. Not feeling a part of anything, they are left with a developmental hunger, which sets them up for an addictive desire to belong to *someone*.

Except the relationships they dream about are fantasies; they're not based on healthy bonds but on psychological bondage. The relationship addict imagines a relationship in which they are in control (the control they never had as a young person), but they are actually lost in their desperation and are out of control. They become emotionally, and even biologically, dependent on another person. Ironically, the dysfunctional nature of this over-dependence means it is pretty much inevitable that they will lose the one person they fear losing the most.

HAND-ME-DOWN BEHAVIOR PATTERNS

Why can't relationship junkies love in ways that don't destroy them and their relationships? We learn early on from parents and parental figures what loving relationships look and feel like. We learn patterns of affection, sexuality, conflict resolution, and especially what we deserve in a relationship from those early family bonds.

I (Sherry) think of my own mother's history of abuse and abandonment. My mother's parents were heavy gamblers, and my grandfather left my grandmother many times throughout my mother's childhood—ultimately divorcing her when my mom was in high school. Having unavailable parents, both emotionally and physically, left a hole in my mother's soul.

She met my father at the young age of seventeen, married soon after, and actually spent close to sixty years mostly happy and fulfilled, until he died. He didn't have any of the irresponsible traits of her parents, and she knew he would take care of her in a way her own parents couldn't. However, when he died, all those buried feelings of being abandoned by her own father came rushing in.

My mother was born at a time when women couldn't imagine life without someone to fill that void. She couldn't tolerate living alone after my father died, so she fell into a relationship with the first man who paid attention to her. She couldn't bear to be without a man—any man. She didn't give herself the time to grieve and get over the pain of losing my dad. Since she had married so young, she'd never actually dealt with being abandoned by her father. She was full of fear and anxiety, and being alone was unbearable.

Her mother did the same thing: After her third husband died, she picked up another gambler at a casino and plunged right back into her relationship addiction. He had nothing to offer her except someone to join her on her gambling trips. When she died of cancer, this man stole everything out of her apartment, leaving nothing behind for her family.

Sadly, when you pick a significant other just so you won't be alone, you are less likely to *really* know who you are sharing your life with. You put aside what is truly important in a partner: someone you can trust, someone you can count on, someone who has your back. My grandmother was willing to tolerate anyone's unacceptable behavior because of her powerful fear of being left alone. Surely, her boyfriend didn't have her back when he stole everything she owned.

Some relationship addicts soothe themselves with other addictive behaviors, such as food, sex, the Internet, shopping, and, in my grandmother's case, gambling. My grandmother had her own abandonment issues; she was raised by a mother who was emotionally unavailable and treated my grandmother like a "little adult" by making her responsible for watching her two younger siblings—who got to be the babies while she had to quickly grow up. She met her first husband when she was sixteen and married him without really knowing who she was or what she wanted or deserved. Her husband also had his own abandonment issues. When his parents came to Canada to escape the anti-Semitism in Europe, they left him behind in Poland, but took their six younger children with them. He was just a little boy at the time and had to wait until they sent for him when he was twelve.

You can see in my family how patterns of behavior and the ways we react to them are passed down through generations. We learn from our parents how to be nurturing or abandoning. We learn from them how to choose partners wisely or foolishly. We learn how to feel safe and fulfilled on our own—or not.

If you are reading this book, you most likely experienced some kind of childhood trauma. You may have been neglected or abandoned or had parents who were abusive and unresponsive to your needs. Perhaps they simply weren't present and that created an emptiness inside of you.

Even the most well-meaning parents may not have given you what you needed due to their own addictions, problems, obligations, or the ways they learned to be in a family and behave as parents. Without love as a child, adults often feel incomplete. One way to fill that hole in your heart is going from relationship to relationship, as I did. You try to use obsessive love to give yourself what you didn't get when you were young.

The problem with this is that your whole sense of self and self-worth rests with someone else. If that person loves you, you are whole, but if they don't, then you are stuck in a hole. It's an endless self-defeating dance of "He loves me; he loves me not."

Every child needs that early nurturing and bonding experience to be able to successfully relate to self and others as an adult. Without it, they feel that they are not enough; they feel they will never have enough. Obsessive love is a subconscious attempt to satisfy that developmental hunger within themselves, that hungry ghost desperate for somewhere to belong, but they look outside themselves to fix what is an inside job.

A WOMAN WITHOUT A MAN

Relationships addicts live by a set of beliefs and rules laid out by parents, friends, and cultural institutions that declare they are not "whole" unless they are in a committed relationship. If you're not, there's something wrong with you.

In *A Gift From the Sea*, Ann Morrow Lindbergh wrote: "How one hates to think of oneself alone. How one avoids it. It seems to imply rejection or unpopularity. An early wallflower panic still clings to the world. One will be left, one fears, sitting in a straight-backed chair *alone*, while the popular girls are already chosen and spinning around the dance floor with their hot-palmed partners. We seem so frightened today of being alone that we never let it happen. . . . When the noise stops there is no inner music to take its place. We must re-learn to be alone."

We live in a world where women are still made to believe they are of less value without a man. It's as if they are half a person without a partner. I (Sherry) chose to be in multiple marriages because I felt deprived and devalued as a woman without a man in my life. I remember when I was raising my daughter always feeling judgment as a single mom and as a woman without a husband. A divorced parent back in the 1980s was not as common as it is today. I remember not feeling like a real a part of the mommy circles. It was as if I had a divorce disease and someone might catch it if they befriended me.

I sometimes think it was the isolation of being a young, single mother that propelled my endless search to fill the empty chair at the dinner table. I would tell myself things like, "If I were really okay, I'd be in a relationship." Anyone could fit the bill, and if he didn't exactly have the traits I was looking for, I could change him. It was as if my happiness depended entirely on another person becoming my fantasy ideal partner.

One of the things relationship addicts do is reshape their partner to match their fantasies of what the perfect partner might be. Sometimes this happens only in their mind; they see what they want to see, rather than what is actually there. Often, that fantasy partner is some version of the person who first abandoned them—the unavailable or neglectful parent or caregiver.

While things have changed a lot for women since the 1980s, they have not changed entirely. There is still pressure to get married, especially if you are dating the same person for a while. Women are repeatedly asked, "When are you getting married?" or "Don't you want to get married?" How many photos have you seen on social media of women showing off their engagement ring? That ring says, "I was picked."

The pressure gets especially strong when a young woman hits her thirties. There is a strong social judgment that by a certain age, one "should be" paired up. After all, their biological clock is ticking. If you are not married by your mid to late thirties, you may have no chance of having a baby. This idea sparks more fear and desperation.

There is a growing proportion of people who are choosing not to marry. In fact, my own daughter is thirty-four, with a little girl, and has chosen not to marry. She is living with her man and her daughter, and is perfectly happy and well adjusted. However, just because you haven't had a wedding doesn't mean you aren't wedded to a relationship. Relationship addiction is not just about marriage.

WHERE FEAR LEADS

Relationship addiction is not about love; it is a desperate search to attach, to belong, and to be connected. It comes from a crippling fear of being alone and abandoned, of not belonging. It is also a delusion that someone will love the addict unconditionally and give them the unlimited attention they so long for. The addiction drives them to obsessively want to be with their love object, in their thoughts and in person.

Underneath all these fears is the fear of the unknown. What if they never find someone to love them? What they need to have a fulfilling life, what they want for themselves, their desires and hopes, are put aside in service of this all-consuming need for connection. This leaves little room for personal growth or self-actualization. For them, it's all about looking for someone else to affirm their worth. The relationship junkie is looking to someone else to complete what's missing within themselves.

A tacit, unspoken agreement takes shape: "If you make me feel secure in this relationship, I will do the same for you and never leave you." If that agreement is broken, or if there is even a hint that it might be, dysfunctional behaviors emerge. One of those behaviors is obsession.

CHAPTER 2

OBSESSION AND ABANDONMENT

The first days of a new relationship are always exciting, even intoxicating. We think about the person we're seeing all the time, wonder what they're doing, whether they're thinking about us, when they're going to call. We imagine them in all sorts of situations with us—fantasize about fun dates, clever conversations, electrifying kisses, and passionate love-making.

It's a delicious paradox of romance that at the beginning, it's always both dangerously sweet (the possibilities) and delightfully painful (the uncertainties). A big part of dating entails figuring out both the possibilities and the uncertainties—weighing the partner and seeing if what you hope for might actually be who they are.

The start of a relationship is always a little bit obsessive because it occupies so much of our thoughts. In healthy relationships, though, after the initial attraction where couples idealize and attach to each other, love matures and changes. As the relationship progresses, we relax and feel more secure; we know our partner loves us, when they will be calling, and what our plans are for getting together. We're a couple. We still think about them often, but it's in a more comfortable way. That "new romance" obsession is gone, replaced by a level of security that can feel just as good in its own way.

Relationship junkies never get past the initial stages of falling in love. They are obsessed with the idea of being in a relationship, no matter what the cost. They don't actually weigh the merits of their partner and honestly evaluate the potential of the relationship. Instead, they become dependent on their partner, hoping somehow this person will complete their lives and create their happily ever after.

The obsessive thinking never goes away. Obsession keeps the relationship addict in fantasy land, enabling them to filter their perceptions through romanticized expectations and dreams. Their new partner is always perfect, always the right one—even if they aren't. The fantasy has little to do with who the person really is, but rather, who the relationship addict needs them to be.

Obsession also forces the addict into endless uncertainty. Relationship junkies live in fear, insecurity, and pain. Obsessive thinking takes on a life of its own, and the addict feels extremely powerless to shape their own future. They are in constant fear that their partner will leave them. The sweetness of possibility is an illusion—a kind of artificial sweetener— and the pain of uncertainty never gives way to comfort and security. This kind of obsession is fueled by fear, and the fear of rejection becomes an obsession—as does the partner who holds rejection at bay. Rejection and abandonment seem like the worst things that could ever happen.

WHAT DOES OBSESSION LOOK LIKE?

The expectations of a relationship junkie are unrealistic, so they are inevitably disappointed. Their relationships are ultimately never truly satisfying, yet they can't live without a relationship because they are so afraid of being alone. Being hooked up with someone relieves these negative feelings, so the addict may use obsessive behavior, such as endless calling, texting, or thinking about the partner, to keep their negative feelings under control.

The relationships of addicts are often dysfunctional and are based more on discomfort, delusion, and obsession than they are on love. *Any* relationship feels better than being single. Because a relationship junkie believes their very survival depends on their partner not leaving, they are hypersensitive to all their partner's behaviors. Any behavior that strays from total attention and devotion makes the addict fearful; small things that really mean nothing take on huge significance. For example, if the partner calls to say they will be late for dinner or are going out with a friend, it's a catastrophe.

One of Sherry's clients, for example, would text her boyfriend several times throughout the day. If he didn't text her back immediately, she would imagine all sorts of dire scenarios—he didn't love her anymore, he didn't want to see her again, he must have met someone else and was leaving her. When Sherry suggested he might be in a meeting and turned his phone off, she rejected the idea. Her obsession always took her thoughts to a much more extreme place.

EXERCISE 1. WHAT ARE YOU THINKING ABOUT?

Certain kinds of thoughts come up in obsessive thinking. These thoughts occur to everyone who is in a relationship, but when you always go there first, when they are pretty much all you think about, when they crowd out all other thinking, they have become obsessive. Obsessive thinking operates in the subconscious and hijacks all logic and reasoning. The mind keeps reliving all sorts of "what happened" and "what if" scenarios, and races with endless fantasies and fears. These obsessive thoughts consume you, and you lose all connection with your true self.

If any of the thoughts listed below sound familiar and you just can't get them out of your head no matter how hard you try, it may be time to consider that perhaps you have your own obsession.

» Constantly reliving the amazing times spent together.

» Wondering what your partner is doing now or whether they are with someone else.

» Visualizing your partner having sexual encounters with others.

» Constantly re-experiencing the intoxicating feeling of their presence.

» Wondering whether your partner is thinking about you.

» Questioning why you are in so much pain and why your partner has not been affected the same way.

» Feeling crazy.

» Planning all the time how you can make a connection with your partner.

» Feeling sick or panicked when you imagine your partner leaving you.

THE NURTURING OBSESSION

Often relationship junkies are drawn to individuals they believe they can save, fix, or change. This is more common for women, who tend to be caretakers, but men can do it too. The reasons are complex. First, the addict believes if they just love this person enough or do enough for them, they will be able to create the relationship of their dreams. The second reason feeds into the insatiable need to be with someone: If you nurture a needy person, they will become dependent on you; and if they are dependent, they will never leave you.

Nurturing someone, helping them to grow and change, is not a bad thing. Often, lovers in a healthy relationship say that over time their partner has helped them become a better person. But just as obsession is love without the sweetness and security, it is also nurturing without the growth. The idea of a nurturing obsession is not to make the addict's partner happier, but to make their partner more dependent. The addict becomes overly responsible for their partner financially, emotionally, and physically, leaving the nurturer (the addict) drained and frustrated. The relationship addict never gets back as much as they give, but keeps thinking that if they give more, they will finally get the fantasy relationship they long for. Since the addict lives in denial, the real problems their partner has are obscured by a cloud of delusion. Relationship junkies refuse to see any reality that threatens to tarnish the image of the person they are obsessed with.

We attract and are attracted to people who share our view of the world. That means people who are willing to give endlessly, often with little in return, tend to attract people who are happy to take endlessly and give back very little. At the very least, relationship addicts end up preventing their partners from growing and making the changes they really need to make. At the very worst, they end up with partners who are charming, manipulative, lying sociopaths.

What makes it even worse is that the addict is blinded by a need to see their partner as they wish to see them. These delusions keep them on an endless quest to save their partner. Often, the partner has a host of problems, but the addict just keeps explaining them away. Do any of these sound familiar?

- » "He's only temporarily out of work."
- » "He is just friends with all his ex-girlfriends."
- » "He only drinks like that because his friends make him."
- » "She's only unavailable emotionally sometimes."
- » "She's just really busy at work."
- » "She's only waiting for the right time to leave her boyfriend/husband."
- » "He only lies sometimes and just to protect me."
- » "She only sometimes tries to change me."
- » "It's for my own good."
- » "When he's jealous, it's because he loves me so much."
- » "When she criticizes me in front of others, it's only because she's trying to help me be better."
- » "He's not controlling, he's concerned about me."

I (Sherry) was one of those people. I married a recovering alcoholic, and although I knew from my work in addiction that relapse is always possible, I chose to file away that knowledge somewhere very deep. After we had been married five years, my husband did relapse. At first, I denied it. As a clinician, I know the signs very well—staying out all night and not calling, smelling like alcohol (and swearing it is cologne), angry outbursts, running out of money, spending more time than usual in the garage—but I just explained them away.

When I could no longer do that, I believed my love alone would save my husband. I put him into rehab several times, only to be disappointed by his continued relapses and his constant lying about it. He never followed up on his promises to go to Alcoholics Anonymous meetings, get a sponsor, or seek therapy. Yet somehow, I continued to believe my love would change him. That was my delusion, and it was born out of my obsession with relationships.

I'm not saying it was a mistake to marry a recovering alcoholic, and I'm not saying all recovering addicts relapse. What I am saying is that I knew when I married him that relapse was a possibility, but when it happened, I ignored the signs. When I could finally no longer ignore them, I deluded myself into thinking I could "love his problem away." I lived in the fantasy that if I could just love him enough, we would live happily ever after. I had already gone through three divorces and couldn't imagine going through a fourth—or being single again.

What I refused to admit to myself at the time was that his disease, his addiction to alcohol, was stronger than anything I could have done to help him. By making excuses for him and supporting him when he could no longer work, I was enabling his addiction. He had relapse after relapse, lied to me about using, and didn't keep his promises. My obsessive love never changed him; and it didn't help him, either.

I knew on some level that I couldn't live like this, going to get him when he was too drunk to get himself home, being gone for days and not knowing where he was, stealing my prescription pills, lying endlessly, and refusing to go to AA meetings or participate in any recovery program. Finally, after so many relapses, I told myself that if he drank again, I would leave him. Relationship addicts often draw these lines in the sand, only to step over them again and again. "This time will be the last time ... no, this time I mean it ... *really*, this is the last time."

Ultimately though, for me, the pain of being a caretaker outweighed my fear of being alone. It took every ounce of strength in me to get there, but I divorced him. However, my obsession to save him did not end with our divorce. I continued to take him to rehab, put gas in his car, buy him food and cigarettes, give him rides, and store his belongings in my garage for three years. But I still wasn't saving him—I was just feeding my obsession and enabling him to keep going in his addiction.

Many obsessive nurturers come from what therapists call a "parentified" family, where needy parents can't meet the emotional and sometimes even the physical needs of their children. The child feels rejected by their emotionally and physically unavailable parents, and believes on some level that they can save their parents. The child becomes the caretaker of the parents as a desperate attempt to keep the parents' attention. This role reversal is common in families where there is neglect, abuse, alcoholism, drug addiction, divorce, or where one parent has died and the remaining parent turns the child into a substitute partner.

When the child grows up, their adult relationships represent the family they grew up in. They are attracted to partners with problems, so that they can finally symbolically fix their parents. They are motivated by the same rejection they endured as children and subconsciously believe they can heal their childhood wounds by nurturing a needy partner. The relationship addict is attracted to the familiarity of this kind of dysfunctional, out-of-balance relationship. People often stick with what they know, and if all they know is dysfunction, they go with it because that's what "normal" seems like.

THE END THAT NEVER COMES

Obsession is what keeps relationship addicts in denial about what is truly going on in the relationship. As the relationship begins to deteriorate, the addict explains, excuses, and justifies their partner's behavior. They rationalize away their pain long after the relationship has soured. There is no letting go easily and peacefully. In fact, there is simply no letting go. They believe that if they are rejected, no one will ever love them again and they will never be able to love anyone else. The prospect of being alone is too terrifying.

Fantasies about the perfect romance keep the relationship junkie in denial, fueling their obsessive thinking. They may obsess about regaining their partner's interest, the heightened passion and sex, the great times, and most importantly the intensity—all the while ignoring the fact that the relationship is falling apart. The addict will not accept the reality that they are in an unhealthy relationship or that it is ending. They may start drinking excessively, overeating, or other addictive behaviors as a way to avoid the pain and suffering of rejection. They are convinced the only way to survive this rejection is to get their partner back—or find someone new to obsess over. Because the fear of being alone is so extreme, they often end up back in the arms of an abusive partner and the cycle begins again.

People in healthy relationships spend some time mourning them when they end, but there comes a point when they move on. Relationship addicts can't stop their obsessive thoughts. The thoughts listed below are normal when a couple breaks up, but if they are constant for you, if they never end and you can't move on, you may be feeling obsessive love fueled by a relationship addiction.

» If only I would have acted this way/said this/did this.

» If only I had handled the situation differently.

» If only I had treated them better.

» I will do anything to get them back.

» I will never love or be loved ever again.

» I will get my revenge.

REVENGE, THE LAST RESORT

Obsession drives a junkie to do anything to maintain a connection with their partner. They send lavish gifts and dozens (or hundreds) of e-mails and texts, call several times a day, and come up with a host of excuses to be near their ex-partner. They may drive by the partner's home or workplace or may even put their parental obligations aside to make contact with them. In extreme cases, this escalates into dangerous stalking behaviors.

If they can't make contact, the obsessive relationship addict may even resort to self-harm as a way to get attention and sympathy. This only further erodes their self-esteem, because the more they pursue the partner, the more they push the partner away. Then the addict feels worse— perpetuating a cycle of pain and shame. As the truth begins to break through their denial, they become angrier at their partner for rejecting them. At this point, a relationship obsession can become an obsession with getting back at the person who has totally ruined their life.

Revenge is usually the last resort for the relationship addict. Some examples include making scenes at their workplace, calling, texting, and e-mailing incessantly, or contacting mutual friends and relatives. They may even destroy personal property, such as homes, cars, furniture, or clothing.

Inflicting pain on their partner is a way to avoid feeling empty, depressed, or abandoned. In reality, it only causes more rejection and pain, restarting the cycle of shame and abandonment. If you have revenge fantasies, this is the time to get professional help from a licensed psychotherapist, sex and love addiction meetings, or a spiritual guide.

BREAKING THE CYCLE OF OBSESSION

When life seems like a choice between living in a kind of fantasy romance novel or the sheer hell of being single, relationship addicts become obsessed with the idea of being in a relationship, no matter what the cost.

In therapy, a client we'll call David told Sherry, "I spent five years in a toxic relationship because the sex was good. I thought that meant the relationship was good, but I ignored problems like lying and cheating (and even drug abuse) for years. I thought I was helping her. One day she got drunk and filed a false police report against me. The cops arrested her instead. I left her and moved to a new city to start over."

Yet David was so uncomfortable without a girlfriend that days after moving he was already agreeing to go on dates with a woman who was interested in him. He never stopped to think about what had gone wrong with his last relationship or even if he really liked this new woman. "She didn't lie or do drugs, and I thought that meant the relationship was good," he said. But he had never actually tried to figure out what kind of relationship might be right for him. To his dismay, his girlfriend could not hold his attention. "I became infatuated with a coworker," he said. "I tried to ignore those feelings, but that didn't work. Over the next few years, my infatuation turned into an obsession. Desperate to stop thinking about her, I decided to swallow my feelings and ask my girlfriend to marry me. Our relationship had serious problems and I didn't want to marry her, but somehow I thought it was the right thing to do." David didn't feel any better after proposing. In fact, he felt worse. He couldn't sleep or eat; he became increasingly stressed and withdrawn. Eventually, he broke off the engagement.

Now it was time to live his fantasy of running away with the coworker he had been obsessing over. "I wrote a messy e-mail to my coworker confessing my feelings," he told me. "She politely rejected me." She'd had no idea David had been fantasizing about her for years. In his mind, he'd built up a whole life for them, but it was all a delusion. David felt so humiliated that he got a different job and moved to a new apartment. He also swore off dating for a year and went into therapy. It was the first step in his process of breaking the cycle of obsession and healing his relationship addiction.

The only way to move through the obsessive thoughts and behaviors is to stay away from the object of your obsession, and the best way to do that is take a break physically. This is a time to focus on the work you need to do, with the goal of healing your addiction, not trying to get your love object back. If you live with the person, you will need to ask him or her to move out, or you may have to stay with friends or get a hotel room or a short-term rental for a few weeks. If you don't live together, there should be no contact at all—in person or through the phone, texting, or e-mailing. We know, going cold turkey is hard, but it's really vital to create the emotional space you will need so you can gain a perspective on your relationship.

It may be the relationship is almost over anyway or is actually done, but you still have obsessive thoughts and behaviors that are making you miserable and crazy. You need a break from your obsessive thoughts and behaviors. It is important to honor your need for this emotional and physical distancing, so you can work on the personal growth you have been avoiding through fantasy and delusion. No one can do this work for you; only you can get it done. If you can't leave your partner or your partner can't or won't leave, then you must get help from a professional psychotherapist to guide you through this process. Remember, the goal is not to get your partner back, but to focus on the changes you are making in your life.

EXERCISE 2. MAKE SOME LISTS

To conquer your obsessive behavior, the first thing you need to do is become aware of it. So much of our behavior is habit, and we do a great many things without thinking. You check your phone dozens of times an hour for texts from your beloved; you conjure up images of them with you—or with others, cheating on you. You're not consciously making a choice to think about this, the thoughts just pop into your head.

The good news is that you can control what you do and even what you think. But first, you need to be aware of it. Sit down someplace private and quiet. Turn off your phone.

Now make a list of all the obsessive behaviors you have engaged in. Here are some possibilities.

- » Stalking in person
- » Texting
- » E-mailing/breaking into their e-mails
- » Telephoning/hanging up
- » Showing up unannounced
- » Stalking on social media
- » Spying
- » Driving by their workplace or home
- » Making contact with their friends or relatives
- » Sending gifts
- » Attempting to get them back after you have broken up
- » Having sex with them after you have broken up
- » Revengeful behaviors
- » Making up excuses to make contact
- » Caretaking behaviors (all the while telling yourself you are "just being nice")
- » Jumping into another relationship

Next, make a list of all the ways you are punishing yourself over this relationship or dealing with your pain in unhealthy ways. This might be:

- » Overeating

- » Drinking
- » Drug abuse
- » Shopping or other addictions
- » Meaningless sex

Take your list of unhealthy behaviors—ways you have acted inappropriately to fill your empty heart—and put them in a column on one side of a piece of paper. Now you are going to replace those behaviors with healthy actions. Opposite each unhealthy behavior, list a healthy activity you can participate in that will nurture your soul—hiking, biking, yoga, dance, painting, cooking, writing, acting, singing, playing an instrument, meditating, volunteering, blogging, or any other pursuits that nurture your spirit. Imagine what it would feel like and look like to have a healthy relationship with yourself. Notice in your body what it would be like to be more connected to healthy pursuits and live a life you love.

The next list, which can be very cathartic, is of all the obsessive thoughts you have been having. Writing them down will help you let go of many of your toxic thoughts. Write in as much detail as possible what those obsessive thoughts are, which ones are the most painful, which ones cause the most fear, and what the triggers are that bring up those thoughts.

Next to each thought, write down the feelings that thought evokes. For example:

- » Sadness
- » Fear
- » Anxiety
- » Shame
- » Rage
- » Trauma
- » Childhood wounds
- » Depression

» Pain

When you let go and allow your mind and body to freely explore these feelings, what's in your subconscious comes bubbling to the surface. See if you can make some surprising connections.

Look at your list of obsessive thoughts. Which ones come from a place of fantasy or denial—"I wonder what it would be like if we got back together" or "I wish he had asked me to marry him." Write down what feelings those fantasy thoughts evoke in you. Is it excitement, passion, or relief? How do those thoughts serve you; what needs do they satisfy?

These exercises can touch at the core of very difficult feelings. While you are doing them, it's a great time to enlist the support of a friend, a 12-step program, a support group, or a licensed psychotherapist to help you deal with the feelings that come up and also to hold you accountable for doing the exercises and embracing the insights they reveal for you. A close friend or sponsor is someone who can call attention to when you are fixating on obsessive thoughts or thinking of obsessive behaviors (like stalking) and remind you not to get stuck.

As you learn to let go of obsessive behaviors and thoughts, you are learning to let go of controlling others. You are learning that you no longer need to be someone's caretaker and that you cannot use a relationship to fix the rejection, abandonment, or neglect from your childhood. Making these lists allows you to pay attention to your own needs, desires, and feelings. Now it's time to put the focus on you and not the object of your obsession.

EXERCISE 3. LET GO OF YOUR FANTASIES

Which of these statements apply to you? Circle all the ones that do.

My partner will:

» Make me feel whole

» Provide constant companionship

- » Fill my emptiness
- » Meet all my needs for connection
- » Provide all the excitement I need
- » Make me feel safe and secure
- » Make me the number one person in their life, even before themselves
- » Prevent loneliness
- » Fix me
- » Expect me to fix them

These kinds of expectations are unrealistic fantasies about what a relationship can and should give you. Believing in unrealistic fantasies will lead you into an unhealthy relationship.

Another common fantasy/obsession is "if only" statements: If only I acted, behaved, or reacted differently, then the relationship would still be perfect. "If only" thoughts are another way of fantasizing about alternative futures with the object of your obsession. They keep you from living in the reality of now and are usually inaccurate. They feed the denial system that keeps you believing the object of your obsession is someone other than who they really are. "If only" thoughts are also a way to avoid facing the uncomfortable truth that the relationship was unhealthy and doomed from the start.

Some examples of "if only" statements:

- » If only he showed me more often how much he loved me, I wouldn't have acted so insecure.
- » If only I hadn't demanded we get married, we would still be together.
- » If only I had acted less available, she would still want to be with me.

These statements are the lies we tell ourselves to avoid dealing with the pain of the relationship ending and the powerlessness we feel about it. "If only" statements don't allow you to examine the roll you play and the reasons why you get tangled up in obsessive relationships. Although, paradoxically, they also leave you with all the blame; only *your* actions matter here. However, because "if only" statements put the blame on you, they also put the power on you. In fact, nothing is further from the truth. Typically, in an obsessive relationship, two individuals with unhealthy needs come together, and the relationship is doomed from the start.

Take a moment to write down the "if only" statements you have obsessed over to avoid your pain or delude yourself. After you have completed your list, look at each statement. Now think—not obsessively, but clearly and honestly—about how your relationship would be "if only" you had handled things differently. (If you're having trouble thinking clearly about this, talk over these statements with a trusted friend or therapist.) Would you have changed? Would your partner have changed? Would the relationship be more loving and intimate, or would it have remained the same? What if you were given the opportunity for a do-over in the relationship? Would you be happy, fulfilled and satisfied, or would the same problems still be there? Would it be as tumultuous, harmful, and painful as before?

When you have finished answering these questions, take some time to reflect on your answers. Do you still notice the same heightened emotions as there were before you started the exercise, or do you feel calmer and less obsessed now?

You need to let go of a fantasy that cannot be fulfilled, because it is a fantasy of who you *thought* your partner was rather than who they really are. Giving up fantasies is difficult and even painful, but a healthy relationship will elude you until you do. The best way to let go of a fantasy is to explore where the fantasy comes from and why you are holding on to it so tightly. Ask yourself the following questions, and you may start to recognize the distinction between what is truth and what is a fairytale offered up by film, television, and romance novels.

» Why am I holding on so tightly to this fantasy?

» What is so alluring about this fantasy?

» Is this kind of perfect partner even possible?

» Where did I learn that I could only be happy if I am in a relationship?

Getting clarity about where your fantasies originate can help you see more clearly why you hold on to them and what it will take to let them go.

EXERCISE 4. GET BACK INTO YOUR OWN LIFE

It may take you a day to complete the previous exercises, or it may take you a week or more. Give yourself the space and the patience to complete them and fully reflect on your answers and the insights you have gained. Once you have done that, it's time to start engaging in life again.

Often relationship addicts isolate themselves from everyone except their obsession—neglecting their friends, giving up activities, and making themselves unavailable for anyone or anything except their partner. Now is the time to change that. Get in touch with friends and family—anyone you have neglected—and make plans to reconnect. Ask them out to dinner or a movie or maybe a day at the spa. Let them know you want to spend quality time with them, not to talk about your ex-partner but to be with them. Go back to activities you put aside—the gym, yoga class, your mahjong game. As you contact old friends and renew activities you have neglected, you will begin to enjoy your own company—perhaps for the very first time.

Getting back to your authentic self allows you to bond with parts of yourself you have disowned or lost because of your unhealthy relationships. These activities are essential to understanding and loving your whole self. You'll see that you can enjoy time with others, as well as time alone. You'll come to realize others can enhance your life, but they can't complete you.

As you push yourself to go out and socialize, as well as spend time alone, you'll begin to feel less dependent on others to make you feel whole.

Understanding your obsessive behavior means facing the loss of the fantasy that somehow the perfect relationship will make you feel complete. Before you can heal, you need to be whole all on your own. Lao Tzu, the Chinese sage, said, "Be really whole and all things will come to you."

Other things you can do to restore wholeness is to buy yourself special gifts, go on a hike in nature, tend your garden, take a nap, draw, paint, get a massage. Try to go back to the simple pleasures you enjoyed before your relationship obsession swallowed up your life. Avoid triggers that remind you of your obsession—restaurants you frequented, photos of both of you, music you listened to together, or anything that connects you with them.

During this time away from your partner, expect to be uncomfortable. You may feel unlovable, unworthy, or defective. These thoughts may become obsessive, and it may seem as if getting back with the object of your obsession will make them stop, but it won't. Give yourself the time to get control of your obsessive thoughts, and you'll have the opportunity to heal and learn how to respect yourself for who you are. While working on this, you may have various symptoms that addicts typically have during the withdrawal stage of an addiction, such as agitation, depression, irritability, and anxiety. Other symptoms might include cravings to act out your obsessions and unhealthy relationship behaviors, physical illness or fatigue, other addictions (alcohol, sex, drugs), indecisiveness, hopelessness, distraction, fear, suicidal thoughts, continued obsessive thinking, anguish, emptiness, shame, fantasies of your partner, mood swings, anger, and confusion.

Be aware of some of the behaviors you may be tempted to use to avoid the pain of being away from your obsession. For example, you may refuse to take a break from your relationship; hook up with people to replace your partner; chase people who are unavailable; fantasize and idealize new prospects without knowing anything about them; or even continue obsessing over the person you are taking a break from. Also, be aware during this break that old wounds from childhood may resurface, along with core fears of abandonment.

If you begin to engage in any of these negative behaviors, first ask yourself: What is it I am running from or to? Am I running from the fear of being alone? Am I running from an empty heart? Am I running from old trauma that is resurfacing?

After you have acknowledged these old addictive and destructive behaviors, take some time and space to just breathe and slow down. Really dive deep to see what is underneath your compulsion to act out. Once you have identified the "why," then ask yourself "how" you can replace these actions with healthier choices. If needed, go back to your list of activities.

EXERCISE 5. POSITIVE AFFIRMATIONS

Positive affirmations are a great way to help banish obsessive thoughts and replace negative thinking with positive thinking. (To learn more about positive affirmations and how to get the most out of them, see the Appendix.) Here are some positive affirmations that will help counter negative, obsessive thoughts. You can also add your own positive affirmations to this list.

I deserve a healthy and fulfilling relationship.

I am growing.

I will get through this break-up from my partner.

I am a worthy person.

I am of value with or without a relationship.

I allow a healthy relationship to come to me.

I can take care of my own wants and needs.

EXERCISE 6. GUIDED VISUALIZATION

Finally, here is a guided visualization that enables you to literally destroy your obsessive thoughts. (To learn more about guided visualization and how to get the most out of it, see the Appendix.)

Imagine your obsessive thoughts are all contained in two large suitcases. Those suitcases are filled with your negative thoughts, resentments, and burdens. Now, pick them up and throw them down a flight of stairs. Watch the suitcases falling down the stairs, then landing on the ground with a huge crash. Notice the relief you feel as these suitcases leave your hands and no longer weigh you down, hold you back, constantly remind you of your obsession.

Look at the suitcases on the ground and feel your anger rise inside you as you remember how those feelings and obsessions have controlled and burdened you. Imagine the suitcases open up, and all those obsessive thoughts start to blow away, never to burden or control you again. Watch all the thoughts swirl in the air up to the sky, up to the sun, and out of sight. Feel the freedom, your shoulders feeling lighter, your breathing easier, and the peace of knowing these obsessions are finally gone.

CHAPTER 3

THE CODEPENDENCY DANCE

Codependency is one of those words that's thrown around so often in so many contexts these days that it seems to lack a specific meaning. We all seem to know codependent relationships are dysfunctional, but "codependent" has now become a synonym for "unhealthy relationship." There are many kinds of unhealthy relationships, and codependency is one of them.

Being dependable is one of those traits that just about everyone is looking for in a partner, a friend, a boss, a parent. There's nothing dysfunctional about being the kind of person others can depend on, or about wanting the people around you to be dependable.

In a healthy relationship, both people depend on each other. That dependence makes the other person feel safe; it nurtures their resourcefulness and resilience. Because your partner is dependable, you feel more fearless, more self-sufficient. They celebrate that strength and independence in you, and you celebrate it in them.

Codependency is not about being dependable; it's about two people surrendering their independence to an unhealthy dependence on each other, which doesn't allow either person to grow. The word itself was originally associated with another kind of addiction: alcoholism. Codependents were enablers—people who made it easier for the alcoholic to live in their addiction by giving them money, buying them alcohol, making excuses for them, taking care of them, or denying their problem.

Why would someone choose to be in a close relationship with an alcoholic and even enable their addiction? As addiction specialists studied these relationships, they found that the enabler was getting as much out of the relationship as the alcoholic. The alcoholic's dependency on the enabler fulfilled their desperate desire to feel needed and valued. As the alcoholic became more and more dependent, the enabler was more and more certain the alcoholic could never leave—thereby guaranteeing the emotional security the enabler craved. Each depended on the other to maintain their dysfunctional lifestyle. They're codependent.

CODEPENDENCY MYTHS AND TRUTHS

Codependency is any relationship in which one partner is unhealthily obsessed with the needs of the other partner, to the point of ignoring their own needs. Codependents look outside their true and authentic self to find happiness and fulfillment, believing it can never come from within.

The word "codependency" has come into mainstream culture with a lot of baggage, but not a lot of specifics. Let's look at a few things that are true and false about codependency. These things are **not true:**

» Codependency isn't a big deal; everyone is supposed to take care of each other.

» Codependency is just a cultural buzzword, not a real psychological condition.

» Codependent relationships only happen with a significant other, such as a boyfriend, girlfriend, or spouse.

» Codependent relationships only happen when one person in the relationship is an alcoholic or drug addict.

» Codependent relationships only happen in the context of abusive romantic relationships.

» Codependents are bad, immature, or emotionally defective.

These things **are true:**

» Codependency can happen in any type of relationship—with your significant other, your children, your boss, your parents, your friends.

» Codependency prevents both people in the relationship from learning and growing.

» Codependency becomes a habit.

» Codependency is progressive; it gets worse over time.

» Codependency can be treated.

ABANDONING THE SELF

What does it mean to abandon yourself? Codependents lose themselves in the life of another person. They attach their core being to the existence of their codependent relationship, and depend on getting approval from someone else for their very identity. They derive their sense of purpose from making sacrifices to fulfill the needs of another, which means they are looking outside of their true and authentic self to find happiness and fulfillment.

One of Sherry's clients was a woman who had survived a childhood of sexual abuse and violence. She suffered from post-traumatic stress disorder, and was in a constant state of anxiety. She used drugs and alcohol to try to tame—or at least numb—the demons from her past. She told Sherry, "That anxiety led me to be completely codependent. The constant trying to control people and situations so I wouldn't get hurt again was exhausting. I would also turn myself inside out to try and make sure I was pleasing everyone around me, thereby losing myself and never finding out what I wanted from life. I was irrelevant."

The codependent only feels good about themselves if they are needed—desperately needed—by someone else. In fact, they want to feel like a martyr, like they're sacrificing themselves for another. Of course, in doing so, they're enabling that person's dysfunctions and preventing them from growing as a person. Enabling the partner's dysfunction is what keeps them dependent—which means they can never leave.

The irony is that codependents can have deep resentments, blaming their partners for the fact that they have lost their identity. It doesn't feel good; there is a profound emptiness in not knowing the reality of who you are because you have no relationship with yourself. Their self is built solely on the relationship, leaving the codependent ultimately feeling lonely, confused, and unappreciated.

CODEPENDENT RELATIONSHIP JUNKIES

Codependency can cause some people to become relationship junkies. However, not all codependents are romance addicts. Remember, we said earlier that codependency can be a part of any relationship—that includes siblings, coworkers, parents, children, and friends. All the things we've been talking about so far can apply to codependent relationships in any of those situations.

Now let's look at codependency in relationship junkies, where the codependent is enmeshed and obsessed with taking care of a romantic partner. This stems from several things: a feeling you alone are not worthy of love, so you must trap or trick someone into staying with you; a frantic need to be in a relationship; and a constant fear of not being able to control the relationship. You know you are in a codependent relationship when you constantly feel insecure, unworthy, and desperate for certainty. You are filled with fear that you will be abandoned or rejected. While in this desperate state, you are hyper-vigilant for signs your relationship is in trouble. There is a constant need for reassurance from your partner that everything is okay. You somehow believe that by sacrificing everything for them, you can control how the relationship will turn out.

Here are some of the signs of codependent relationship addicts:

- » Fear of being alone
- » Fear of being rejected
- » Feeling anxious when alone
- » Using alcohol, drugs, shopping, eating, gambling, or the Internet to keep from being alone
- » A relationship is your "drug" of choice
- » Feeling that you are not enough
- » A damaged relationship with yourself
- » Clingy, suffocating, controlling, demanding, or manipulative behavior
- » Being overly emotional or melodramatic
- » Always needing reassurance
- » Terrified of being wrong and unable to forgive yourself if you are wrong
- » Afraid of being right because it might cause conflict with your partner
- » Feeling you cannot disagree, out of a fear of displeasing your partner
- » Feeling you're not worthy to have a different opinion
- » You don't take the initiative due to fear of failure
- » You say "yes" when you mean "no"

As you think about this list, it is clear that codependent relationship junkies lose themselves within the relationship.

WHY DO WE DO THIS?

No surprise—codependency is the result of a childhood full of unmet needs. The codependent believes that if they sacrifice enough, their partner will give them everything they didn't get as a child.

Codependent adults grew up in families where there was not a lot of nurturing. It's more common in children of alcoholics, drug addicts, and abusers, but lack of nurturing can occur in all kinds of families and in all kinds of ways. These parents give their children the message that what the parents need and want is more important than what the children need and want. When the children demand care, the parents either don't respond, or respond by telling them they are selfish or undeserving, or with verbal or even physical attacks. The children then feel guilty about asking for care.

Typically, these kinds of needy parents express love for their children only when the children are taking care of the parents. The dynamic here is that to be loved, to be a good person, you must take care of others and ask nothing in return. The codependent learns to rescue others as they once tried to rescue their parents.

When children aren't nurtured or cherished as individuals, it creates feelings of abandonment, helplessness, isolation, and hopelessness. The real self isn't seen or isn't valued. While a healthy, nurtured child becomes confident and proud of who they are, a neglected child becomes ashamed of who they truly are and buries their authentic self, the self that they believe is just not good enough. A neglected child projects a false self—the person they think they must become in order to get what they need. They become further and further removed from their true self and more convinced that if they can just give up enough of themselves, they will finally be loved. Codependency thrives in this shame-filled, inauthentic, desperate space.

At the bottom of codependency is extreme giving to others to get love and acceptance and to feel needed. Codependents expect others will be grateful for all this selflessness, and if others are not, they feel resentful and unappreciated. Rather than leaving the relationship, though, they try harder.

MANIPULATION AND CONTROL

At the core of this negation of self is fear. Codependents are afraid they will be "exposed," that people will see how unlovable they really are and abandon them. They're afraid to make a mistake, afraid to be less than perfect, afraid they'll never be enough. Even as they bury their authentic selves, they are afraid of losing their identity.

Codependents are also afraid to be alone; they need constant affirmation and companionship. They need to be needed because they believe someone will stay with them only if that person is dependent on them. A codependent doesn't trust themselves, but they're not comfortable trusting others either because no one has ever been truly trustworthy in their lives. This means they never really feel safe. To ward off the danger they feel all around them, they develop routines, traditions, and rules. Control—of people and situations—is their primary way to hold back the fear. They feel as if their lives are out of control, but they hide it from others and even from themselves. In fact, they've had a lifetime of practicing how to look like they're in control when they feel out of control. Codependents learned early on how to appease and manage their parents, and they end up trying to manage all the people around them—especially their romantic partner.

Due to their desperate need to be the person others depend on, and because they encourage their partner to be dependent on them, at their best they look like the strong one, the capable one, the reliable one. But at their worst, they can seem manipulative and controlling.

EXERCISE 1. AM I DOING THE CODEPENDENCY DANCE?

Once again, it's time for some tough questions. Remember to be as honest as you can. Codependents have spent a lifetime denying their reality. Now it's time to finally face yours. Remember to be gentle with yourself. You're asking these questions to help yourself, not to be hurtful or to shame yourself.

Circle the statements that describe your present behavior or your behavior in a past relationship.

1. I seldom make enough time to do things just for myself.

2. I would never feel comfortable taking a vacation by myself.

3. I am not really satisfied with the number and kinds of relationships I have in my life.

4. I am not comfortable letting others into my life and revealing the real me to them.

5. I find it's best not to tell someone they bother me because it will only cause fights and make everyone upset.

6. I am aware that I often look happy when I really feel sad.

7. I wish I could accomplish a lot more each day.

8. I hold back my feelings most of the time because I don't want to hurt anyone.

9. When a close friend or relative asks for my help, I say "yes" even when I really want to say "no."

10. I find it difficult to be alone.

11. I tend to think of others more than myself.

12. People seem to admire me because I am so understanding of others, even when they do something that annoys me.

13. I do more than my share of the work.

14. I have sex when I do not want to or when I am feeling hurt and angry.

15. It is hard for me to talk to someone in authority (boss, teachers, etc.).

16. I have trouble getting out of a relationship that becomes confusing and complicated.

17. I feel embarrassed by the behaviors of those close to me.
18. I often waste a lot of time and don't get anywhere.
19. I feel confused about who I am and where I want to go in my life.
20. I have difficulty handling my problems calmly and directly.
21. I don't make major decisions easily.

If you have circled:

1–4 statements, you have problems setting boundaries

5–10 statements, you show codependent traits

11 or more statements, you are doing the codependency dance

WHAT DOES THE OTHER PERSON GET OUT OF IT?

Why would someone stay in a relationship with a desperate, controlling, over-emotional, inauthentic person? We said the codependent feels best when they are making extreme sacrifices to accommodate the needs of their partner. This leaves them vulnerable, because they lose the ability to accurately judge people and situations. They easily fall prey to self-centered and self-consumed partners, such as addicts and narcissists. Without having a sense of their authentic self, codependents do not have the ability to pick healthy partners for whom give and take is a normal part of a relationship.

Remember, we said codependents used to be called enablers. They enable their partner to be as self-indulgent, irresponsible, emotionally withholding, and unhealthy as they want. The enabled partner may appear powerless because they depend completely on the enabler. In fact, the enabled one holds all the power, because they can emotionally blackmail the enabler with the threat of abandonment if they don't get exactly what they want. The enabled partner has become just another version of the codependent's un-nurturing parents.

While each is giving the other what they crave, neither one is actually getting what they need. The codependent may be enabling their partner's addiction, poor physical or mental health, lack of initiative, immaturity, laziness, irresponsible behaviors, lying—or all of those. That may make things easier in the short run, but in the long run the enabled partner will never grow up and become an independent, well-functioning person. This codependent relationship will become stifling for both parties.

The bottom line is codependents seek someone to nurture them the way their parents never did, but they attract self-centered partners. In a codependent relationship, neither person will ever get what they need because there is no dignity in a relationship in which both partners are unable to disengage when it is obvious the relationship is no longer working. They are setting themselves up for failure right from the start.

HOW TO STOP DANCING

You can never actually remake someone into the person you want them to be. Instead, you have to be your true self—and so does your partner. Becoming a healthy adult means learning to let go of all the toxic lessons from your childhood and learning how to live independently so that you can one day live interdependently.

That's a painful route for most of us, and we have learned that painful feelings are bad, but at the bottom of pain is where we find insight. Pain is the doorway to healing. If we are open to the pain, we will hear messages from the deepest parts of us that can save our lives and bring peace and healing.

The codependency dance is a dance of fear, insecurity, shame, and resentment. We need to teach ourselves the dance of power, courage, and determination. It's a dance about honoring your own values and letting the desperation go. When you know your own worth, you are more able to be autonomous and less vulnerable to falling into a codependent relationship.

The goal is not to make someone so dependent on you that they will never be able to leave. The goal is to seek an open, honest, and compassionate relationship with healthy boundaries where both people take care of their own needs and the needs of their partner.

Your partner can never give you everything you didn't get as a child, because your childhood is your past. You can't go back there. It's important to acknowledge the neglect or abandonment you felt as a child, but at the same time to let go of that child-like part of yourself. Think about accepting and healing those early wounds, rather than using them as a reason to seek out or stay in an unhealthy relationship.

Releasing codependency is all about unearthing the authentic self that has been shrouded in shame and fear. By releasing those old wounds, you release the need to control others—and their ability to control you.

EXERCISE 2. POSITIVE AFFIRMATIONS

Getting out of a codependent relationship can be terrifying because of all the fear that goes into them. These positive affirmations can help you feel powerful and worthy enough to begin to let go. (To learn more about positive affirmations and how to get the most out of them, see the Appendix.)

The only thing I lose when I let go is fear.

I am more powerful than anything that frightens me.

I let go of my codependent past and am free to live positively in the present.

I am not my codependent past.

Letting go does not mean giving up.

CHAPTER 4

SETTLING FOR LESS

We all tend to pick partners who reflect the vision we have of ourselves and our world. Unfortunately, that means relationship junkies end up being attracted to partners who remind them of their dysfunctional family relationships, where they never got what they needed. It's ironic, in a way, because while they're searching for someone to be their everything, they end up settling for much, much less.

Here are some of the reasons relationship addicts settle for partners who just don't give them what they need.

- » **Denial.** Denial of reality keeps us deluding ourselves about who someone really is. We see only what we want to see.

- » **Illusions.** We believe we can change people into who we want them to be. We assume they will somehow behave differently with us or that we can make them behave differently. We might convince ourselves that once we're married, they will miraculously become the person we long for them to be.

- » **Low self-esteem.** High self-esteem is a result of empathic and nurturing parenting, but if we grow up in a family where our needs are not met, validated or acknowledged, we feel invisible and believe our needs don't matter. This can result in feelings of unworthiness and not being good enough because we have been invalidated and misunderstood.

» **Shame.** Underneath shame are deep feelings of self-deprecation and inadequacy. We feel unworthy, unlovable, and disconnected from ourselves—and therefore, others. When feelings of shame push us into low self-esteem, we end up sabotaging our relationships with controlling, rescuing, and/or people-pleasing behaviors.

» **Dependence.** An unhealthy attachment to another person is not the same as a healthy connection with someone who is dependable. In essence, we cannot recognize our wholeness and completeness, so instead we enter into relationships as half a person—someone who feels incomplete without a partner.

» **Emptiness.** This feeling is a result of growing up in a family where our need for nurturing and empathy was not met. If our basic need for attachment is not met, the resulting feelings of abandonment set us up for depression, anxiety, chronic loneliness, and isolation—all aspects of emptiness or a feeling of nothingness.

» **Fear of abandonment and rejection.** Missing out on early bonding with a primary caregiver can cause extreme fear of abandonment. A child being "parentified"—taking on responsibilities way beyond what they are developmentally able to handle—can also cause fear of abandonment. When these children become adults, they continue the abandonment cycle by either having relationships with people who are emotionally unavailable or by avoiding relationships entirely—thereby eliminating the threat of rejection.

For some or all of these reasons, we end up choosing partners who are emotionally, physically, and/or spiritually unavailable. We pick partners out of desperation, exposing ourselves to relationships filled with control, jealousy, and anger. Which, of course, makes it impossible to be in a fulfilling, intimate, and meaningful relationship.

These choices fulfill a subconscious need to pick partners who remind us of the dysfunctional parent-child bonds we are so familiar with. We believe we will fix old childhood wounds by picking these familiar partners. In other words, we'll marry someone who is just like mom and dad (demanding, un-nurturing, unresponsive to us), but this time they will give us just what we need. We'll get to live our childhood over, but this time with a happy ending.

But this idea is a fantasy, and, as we have seen, we end up trying to change our partner and control the relationship—without success. If our parents disappointed us and we marry someone who is just like our parents, that person will also disappoint us.

When we're disappointed, though, rather than move on, we start making excuses for our partner. When we deny what is real in a partner, we lose the ability to assess who we are picking and become more vulnerable to being abused by our partners, both emotionally and physically. When we cling to another out of fear of abandonment and deep-seated feelings of emptiness, we attract the sort of person who takes rather than gives. This reinforces the idea that we are unworthy of love and respect in a relationship—but we will only get as much love as we believe we are entitled to. By lowering our standards in picking a partner, we minimize our own worth and integrity.

"He is not the man for me," a client once told Sherry. "I wish I could leave him, but I am stuck. I love him and hate him, so I guess I will have to stay." That is the essence of settling for less.

BUYING INTO THE FANTASY

All these forces that influence our bad choices are happening in our unconscious mind. They sabotage our choices with powerful messages that we are not even consciously aware of. The way to make better choices is to bring these influences into the conscious mind, where we can examine them and figure out what isn't working. It's time to ask ourselves some hard questions. As we mentioned in the Introduction, it's important to answer them all. It may be helpful to meditate or to pray on these questions, letting the answers come to you and being open to whatever you discover.

» Why do you continue to stay in unhealthy relationships when you know that what's in it for you is so much more negative than positive?

» Is something keeping you stuck in the relationship?

» Do you get hooked on the illusion of who you think your partner is (or could be), rather than accepting the reality of the situation?

Women, especially, are really good at lying to themselves, and do so over and over again, so they can cling to a fairytale illusion of their partner. The lies we tell ourselves and others begin to sound believable as we desperately try to convince everyone that we are happily in love. It becomes easier to deceive ourselves than to face the truth. We cling to romantic notions of what love "should" feel and look like and ignore our intuition when reality doesn't align with our fantasy.

Friends and family members ask why we stay with "that guy," and it's embarrassing to admit that we feel like we need a man—any man—to survive and feel comfortable in our own skin. It's easier to just avoid the truth than to fess up and face our demons. So we end up living on autopilot, deliberately unconscious to the reality of who our partner truly is and how they really treat us. We make excuses for unacceptable behaviors, such as physical or emotional abuse, infidelity, addiction, and financial dependence. We sugarcoat everything on the outside so that we can feel safe and secure on the inside. We keep ourselves busy with outside activities, we self-medicate with food, alcohol, shopping, and whatever else we need to avoid feeling the emptiness and disappointment deep within our core. We ignore the warning signs that we are in an unhealthy relationship. We believe the old adage that love can conquer all. When our partner disappoints us—which they will—we get angry, but still we stay.

Some more hard questions to ask yourself:

» What lies have you been willing to tell so you don't have to face your own emptiness and fear of abandonment?

» When have you twisted the truth about your unhealthy relationship?

» What realities have you faced, only to turn around and bury yourself back in the fairytale?

» What motivates you to stay in an unhealthy relationship? Is it fear of abandonment or rejection? Is it a desire to fit in to what you believe society or your family expects of you?

» What would being alone to face your demons feel like? What keeps you from going there?

Women have been hearing for centuries that they are somehow "less than" without a man. As we discussed in chapter 1, these lies are perpetuated in books, magazines, film, TV, and our social institutions. Ask yourself:

» What myths and fantasies have I bought into from popular culture of what it means to be a single person and what it means to be in a relationship?

» How often have I lied to myself, believing I can change or fix my partner?

» How often have I told myself I will somehow be different than all the other women who have tried to fix him?

CAN WE REALLY FIX SOMEONE?

Whenever we focus on fixing someone else an alarm should go off, because what that really means is that there is something inside of us that needs to be addressed. Focusing on another person is just a way to avoid focusing on ourselves and our issues.

The truth is, you are powerless to change anyone except yourself, and you are kidding yourself if you think otherwise. Only your partner can change themselves, and only if they really want to change. If you keep making it easy for your partner to exploit you, they've got no reason to change.

How often have you told yourself that if/when you get engaged/married/move in together, things will change? Think about this honestly: Have you ever really seen someone change just because they ended up living together? If they weren't working on their issues before making a commitment, they won't be working on them after. Don't waste your time believing "If he loves me he will . . ." or "If I'm just more patient he will . . ." These are the things that happen in romantic movies and novels, but they don't actually happen in real life.

Sometimes you may see minor changes, but these are usually short-lived. Typically, these changes are based on your partner's own fears—or they're a way to manipulate you. For example, when my fourth husband and I separated, he would promise he'd go to 12-step meetings and get a sponsor. He would go to meetings, but only a few, and that was usually followed by a relapse. Those short-term changes were his way of manipulating me to let him back into my life. I would hold on to hope when he kept his promises, however briefly, only to be disappointed when he didn't keep it up.

What I have learned from this experience is that we need to accept our partners where they are, or leave them. There are some issues that are deal breakers and others you can accept. If you decide you can't accept something, move on, or else you will live in a constant state of resentment and anger. Trying to change someone is an attempt to control them. A person has to *want to* change for it to be lasting change, and they have to do the work; it takes rigorous honesty, self-reflection, and a willingness to transform for real change to take place.

Think about your own life and how difficult it has been to change. What makes you think it will be any easier for your partner? The bigger question is why do you need someone to change for you? Shouldn't they want to change for themselves? Wouldn't it be better to be with a partner who is on their own self-reflective path?

Ask yourself:

» How often have I tried to fix someone to make them into who I want them to be?

» Can I really help them be "the best version of themselves" if they don't want to change?

» How does this make me feel about myself?

SEPARATING POTENTIAL FROM THE PRESENT

How often have you gotten into a relationship with "potential"? I (Sherry) did this with every marriage I entered in to. When I met my fourth husband, I knew he was a recovering alcoholic who was new in his sobriety. Programs like Alcoholics Anonymous advise their members not to get into a relationship until they've spent at least a year in a recovery program and have been sober the entire time. I met my then-husband-to-be after he had only two months of sobriety. He was in no position to commit to me, and I certainly was in no position to commit to him, but I believed in his "potential."

Even though I am a licensed psychotherapist and on some level understood we were entering a committed relationship way too soon, I deluded myself into thinking our situation was somehow different. I knew his relapse was a real risk, but I just could not be honest with myself, because if I did, I would have had to walk away from the relationship— which I was afraid to do.

Underneath that mountain of lies and denial, though, we all have the wisdom of our intuition. We just choose to ignore it. The realities we push away are the very things we should be listening to because somehow, deep down inside, we know what's true. At the beginning of this chapter, we suggested you might want to meditate or pray on the questions we posed. These are both ways to tap into the wisdom of your intuition—to scrape away the denial and shame and illusion and get to the truth.

Once we started dating and getting serious, he stopped going to AA meetings and didn't have a sponsor or a recovery plan. I knew it was a recipe for a relapse, but I told myself a huge lie—that he had already hit bottom once and would never let that happen again. In fact, seven years into our marriage, as I mentioned, he did relapse. My inner wisdom, my intuition that I repressed, knew the truth all along, but I had refused to listen to it.

What keeps us from listening to our intuition and picking a partner in the present, rather than picking them for what we believe is their potential? Ask yourself:

» When have I picked a partner because I am in love with their potential rather than who they are right now?

» What were the results of getting involved with potential?

» When have I settled for a partner who was willing to make small, minor changes, believing they would inevitably transform themselves?

» What happened eventually with those small changes? Did they turn into a complete transformation?

» When have I allowed romantic illusions to shut out the truth of who someone really is?

» When have I let romantic words or gestures (being told, "You are my one and only," "I will love you forever," or "You are the only one for me") cloud my judgment? How have these romantic gestures kept me from seeing the person for who they really are?

» When have these romantic gestures fed a deep longing inside me that I believe can only be filled by a relationship?

AVOIDING LOVE AVOIDERS

Relationship addicts and love avoiders find each other by an almost magnetic attraction, Love avoiders are disconnected from themselves and their feelings. They enter relationships with their walls up and don't allow anyone in—which makes an intimate relationship impossible. Usually, they are focused almost obsessively on work, a hobby, sex, substance abuse, or something else that always takes precedence over their partner.

Relationship junkies are often attracted to these emotionally unavailable partners. They are attracted to each other because both have experienced childhood abandonment and loss and they share the same attachment issues, but they deal with them in different ways. The addict needs an all-consuming love, but they end up with someone who prefers to avoid real love entirely. Talk about a recipe for disaster!

Relationships addicts want to remain in a relationship at any cost. Love avoiders' favorite aspect of the relationship is the chase; it makes them feel desirable and in control. When they have landed their prey, the game is no longer fun, so they distance themselves emotionally and want to end things.

Relationships addicts want to control the relationship so they can never be abandoned, but love avoiders are very fearful of any type of control. Just like romance junkies, love avoiders fear being abandoned, but they counter that fear by leaving the relationship first—before someone leaves them. Their idea of avoiding abandonment is to never really get involved in the first place.

Love avoiders will do anything to avoid the shame and worthlessness they feel if they are the one who is left. They are experts at avoiding being abandoned; they belittle, criticize, and verbally, or sometimes even physically, abuse the relationship addict to create distance and push them away. The relationship junkie puts up with this behavior because they have such a high tolerance for neglect and abuse. They will often put up with lying and cheating because of their deep fear of a break-up, while the love avoider keeps doing their best to sabotage the relationship.

And so the duel for control plays out. The love avoider maintains control by steering the relationship toward a break-up. The relationship addict then comes up with all sorts of controlling, manipulative techniques to avoid a break-up. They will play the helpless damsel in distress, nag, use guilt or jealousy or try to make their partner dependent on them, all so the partner won't leave. It's the worst kind of relationship, because neither partner feels safe or happy or cared for. Both are terrified, both are insecure, and both are trying to manipulate the relationship in unhealthy ways.

Underneath all this behavior, the love avoider and the relationship addict both feel a profound sense that they are unworthy and unlovable. Neither is their authentic self; neither can create authentic love.

A relationship addict who worked with Sherry described her years of attracting love avoiders. "My idea of being in a relationship was to give my entire self to the other person. When they treated me badly, which is what happened all the time, I would find more of myself to give. I made myself too available to anyone who showed interest in me. That interest usually came in the form of them being physically attracted to me. I learned from a very early age that I was valued most for my appearance. My talents, intelligence, compassion, and ability to love unconditionally was something that didn't feature high on the reasons to date me or even to love me. My relationships were with men who were emotionally, mentally, and physically abusive. Once they got tired of me sexually, I was tossed aside mercilessly. It has taken years of therapy to realize the part I played in attracting these types of men. Because of chronic low self-esteem and feeling I was worthless, anything that looked like love was acceptable to feed my empty heart and soul. I so badly craved healthy love from my father, and when I didn't receive that I set about looking for that love from men who behaved just like him."

LOVING A NARCISSIST

Sometimes people who are bad for us seem exciting in a kind of dangerous way. Sometimes they start out by doting on us, but then change their tune once we've been hooked. And sometimes we make ourselves vulnerable because we put up with too much and then stay too long in a relationship, even when things have soured. All three happen when someone desperate for a partner falls for a narcissist.

When we think of narcissism, we think of someone who is self-centered, egocentric, lacks empathy, and always has to be right. A little touch of narcissism is necessary for our self-esteem, but when the relationship addict falls for a true narcissist, they have entered into the most toxic relationship of all.

The Mayo Clinic research group defines narcissistic personality disorder as "a mental condition in which people have an inflated sense of their own importance, a deep need for excessive attention and admiration, troubled relationships, and a lack of empathy for others." To understand the narcissist, you have to understand the roots of their disorder. In early childhood, they were not nurtured in a way that made them feel cared for and safe. They feel so insecure and unworthy that they over-compensate by creating a false persona—one who gets everything they want, the instant they want it. This is the exact opposite of who they really were as children.

How do you know you're dating a narcissist? Narcissists often:

» Compliment you in a way that actually makes them seem more desirable. ("You're so beautiful that all my friends will be jealous," sounds like it's about you, but really, it's about them.)

» Love to dominate a conversation, mostly talking about how great they are.

» Put others down to make themselves feel better.

» Seek instant gratification and react badly when you don't give them what they want.

» Have a sense of entitlement and believe the rules don't apply to them.

» Seem charming and make lots of promises, but don't follow through and aren't dependable.

Narcissists project a superiority complex, but deep down they actually feel inferior. They feel a huge void, and they must fill it up with adoration, praise, and love from others. But it doesn't matter how much love and attention you give a narcissist; they will always feel empty. Their relationships are just a means to an end, a way to try to fill their emptiness. True intimacy is impossible because that would mean dropping the persona and being seen for the unworthy person that deep down they feel they are.

There are three stages to most narcissistic relationships. In the first stage, the narcissist chooses their prey based on what that person can do for them in terms of building up their self-esteem. Narcissists will choose successful and attractive individuals because dating a desirable person makes the narcissist look more desirable. They are often charming, and in the beginning, they will dote on their love object, putting them up on a pedestal and chasing them almost addictively. This is exactly what the relationship addict falls for, because it meets their insatiable need for acceptance and validation.

Once the narcissist has conquered the object of their desire, the second stage begins. The pedestal breaks, and the narcissist starts blaming their partner for every tiny hiccup in the relationship, becoming overly critical and moody. This is an attempt to avoid bonding, something they secretly fear. The narcissist picks fights and creates problems. They build an emotional wall around themselves so no one can truly know them or get close. The relationship addict will likely be dazed and confused, not knowing what has happened and desperately wanting to go back to the stage where they were being worshiped and adored.

Finally, during the last stage of the relationship, the relationship addict keeps obsessively giving and giving in a desperate attempt to get that original addictive attention back. When you settle for someone who is a narcissist, you end up denying your own needs and just wanting to make your partner happy. But it's no use; the narcissist leaves anyway. They always do.

If you have a constant need to be adored, you're an easy target for a narcissist, who has a constant need to be revered. But neither partner will ever get what they need in that kind of a relationship because their needs are, literally, insatiable.

This situation is more dangerous for the relationship junkie than it is for the narcissist, because the addict gives their partner the power to determine their worth. Deep down, the narcissist is broken and powerless, but they turn their insecurities back on the relationship junkie. The partner is assigned all the negative character traits that the narcissist is unwilling to own. The narcissist does this by attacking, demeaning, and criticizing their partner—and occasionally throwing a bone of attention and adoration to the relationship addict to reel them back in.

The relationship addict, with their weak boundaries, will tolerate behaviors they never thought they would. Over and over, they will try to prove their love and devotion to the narcissist, who knows the more the relationship focuses on them, the more dependent and powerless they will become. It doesn't matter how degrading the situation becomes because now the addict has lost the power to leave.

One particularly insidious behavior narcissists use to keep relationship addicts dependent on them is offering unsolicited help, making the addict believe they aren't capable of dealing with their own issues. This keeps the addict attached to the very end, believing they will receive the love, safety, and protection they so desire. An elderly client of Sherry's who was in a relationship with a narcissist believed she couldn't move into her new home by herself. While they were courting he found a way to move right in with my client by offering to help her pack, hang up pictures, and rearrange the furniture. His plan was to use these nice things as a way to get her to depend on him and have her invite him to move in—which she did. After he moved in, he began to take control of her life, and my client became more and more dependent on him. He started cooking for her, taking her to doctor appointments, isolating her from her friends, and even talking negatively about her family. She deluded herself into thinking he was being kind and giving, but in reality, he had ulterior motives of taking over her life and financial affairs—all part of his narcissistic plan.

It is very rare for a narcissist to make any effort to change their behavior, because this personality disorder prevents them from seeing themselves as anything but superior and justified. The only solution is to leave. But it's not easy to get away from a narcissist, especially for a relationship junkie. Without psychotherapy and/or support from a 12-step program, the relationship of a relationship junkie and a narcissist will become more and more unsafe and addictive. Over time, with the right kind of help, the relationship addict can reevaluate their misconceptions and misunderstandings of themselves and of the narcissist.

It is very common for the narcissist to actively undermine the efforts of their prey to gain strength and change their behavior. Yes, they will eventually end the relationship, but it can only be on their terms. As they see changes in their partner, the narcissist may become more abusive, fear abandonment, and go back to the original seductive, charming behavior to try to stop their partner from leaving. It will be critical for the relationship addict to see this behavior for what it is—an escalation in narcissism. Psychotherapy, support groups, and reliable friends are all important parts of breaking away from that pattern.

Loving a narcissist is an attempt to try to heal parts of yourself that are unhealed. That's why it is so important to own all of you—even the parts that are not yet quite whole. Find a way to re-parent yourself and give yourself those things you never received early on (more about this in chapter 6). Reevaluate your beliefs about what healthy love might look like. Ask yourself:

» What unhealed parts in my life allowed me to attract a narcissist?

» What early childhood wounds need to be explored?

It is important for the relationship addict to create boundaries to keep safe from the narcissist and to learn how to allow people into their space who are reliable and are not in the relationship only for themselves. (More about setting healthy boundaries in chapter 9.) They need to boost their self-esteem, so they aren't dependent on another person to provide them with a sense of worthiness and self-confidence.

WHY DO WE PICK THE WRONG PARTNERS?

What is it about women, especially, that we settle for less or believe having someone (anyone) is better than having no one? How many friends do you know who have gotten married with this attitude, only to end up in divorce court? In my practice, I (Sherry) have noticed many women settle because they believe time is running out for having children or fear that all the available men out there prefer to marry younger women, or are afraid the pool of available men is dwindling. These women would do a lot better if they looked inward to understand why they are attracting the wrong guys—or perhaps appreciated the time alone for personal growth.

» What self-limiting beliefs have you held on to—that there aren't enough men to go around or that perhaps you are too old to attract anyone?

» Have you ever told yourself that what you truly desire doesn't exist and you will never find a better partner than whoever you are with now—no matter how unhappy that person makes you? Why do you believe that?

» Have you ever told yourself that no one will ever want you because you are not thin enough, young enough, don't make enough money, or have too much emotional baggage?

» What social norms are you buying into that are keeping you frozen in the belief that you must be paired up with someone?

» Are you comparing your life with others? Do you live in the illusion that they must be happier because they are in a relationship and you're not?

» When did getting a romantic partner become more important than self-respect?

So many clients I have worked with compare themselves to their friends who are dating, moving in together, getting married. They spend all their time future-tripping about the spouse, the house, the children. They live in a fantasy future and forget to pay attention to who they are picking in the present as a partner. When we aren't honest about what motivates us, we end up settling for less every time. What motivates you to rush into what should be careful, thoughtful choices?

» Are you looking for security and safety?

» Is your fear keeping you stuck in the wrong relationship?

» What would your life look like if you made a decision based on self-worth and self-esteem and a belief that you deserve the very best life has to offer you?

» What would your life look like if you waited just a little longer for the right partner?

Really take a moment, slow it down, and check in about what motivates you to push at life rather than letting it naturally flow. What stories are you creating? The truth is that you deserve to find a relationship that is the right fit for you and only you. Never mind what anyone else is doing with their life. Never mind what everyone else is telling you.

Stop settling for less and expecting another person to make you feel whole. You are whole just as you are in this moment. Declare right now that you deserve the very best. Promise yourself that you will begin to check your motivations, not compare yourself to others, get involved with someone for the right reasons, and deserve everything in a partner that you desire.

EXERCISE 1. JOURNALING

This journaling exercise helps you see your past and guides you to make different choices. Think about each of these statements and write down whatever comes to mind. Just write as you think; what you write doesn't need to be organized or have perfect grammar—it just needs to be honest.

Read what you've written and think about it. How can you change these unhealthy patterns? (To learn more about journaling and how to get the most out of it, see the Appendix.)

1. I pick unavailable partners.
2. My partner is afraid of commitment.
3. I picked a married person to have an affair with.
4. My partner only thinks about himself or herself.
5. I pick abusive partners.
6. My partners have been addicts (substances, Internet, food, gambling, work, etc.).
7. I am attracted to love avoiders.
8. I have imagined a relationship where there has not been one.
9. I see a pattern in my relationships.
10. Do I know what a healthy relationship might look like?
11. Do I know why I make the choices I make?

CHAPTER 5

BREAKING UP IS HARD TO DO

However you got here—whether your partner broke up with you or you decided to break it off—this time is going to be different. After all the work you've done so far, you know that your worth, your identity, your very being does not depend on just one person. This time, you're not going to focus all your energy on getting that partner back, on beating yourself up, or on finding someone else as quickly as you can. This time, you will take time to work all the way through the grieving process and come out the other side stronger and smarter.

In 12-step programs—the kind designed to support addicts who are leaving behind substance addictions like alcohol and drugs, or process addictions like gambling—it's vital for members to totally avoid the object of their addiction. So not even a little glass of wine, not even a single puff of marijuana, not even a church bingo game.

Whether they need to avoid those things forever is actually a matter of disagreement and even some controversy. Traditional programs like Alcoholics Anonymous say a lifetime of abstinence is the only way to control an addiction, while other programs say some people can slowly incorporate some activities back into their life, in moderation. However, everyone agrees that to kick an addiction, you must start with a period of total abstinence. That goes for relationship junkies too. Your brain needs time to adjust (remember what we said in chapter 1 about how addiction affects the brain chemistry), and your body needs time to heal. Your spirit needs healing time as well. You need to learn new habits, new ways of thinking about yourself and about relationships. But first you need to grieve.

GRIEF IS A PROCESS

Psychologists say that grief—or any kind of loss, from a parent to a pet to a house to a relationship—occurs in stages. Five stages of grief were first proposed by Elisabeth Kübler-Ross in her 1969 book *On Death and Dying*. These stages are denial, anger, bargaining, depression, and acceptance. People who are grieving do not necessarily experience all of these stages, and they don't happen in the same order for everyone. Ultimately, grief is as individual as we are. But these five stages are a good framework for helping us untangle the many emotions that arise and understand what we are experiencing when we grieve for a relationship.

In the beginning stages, grief is an overwhelming time of great emotional pain. You might feel numb and clouded; everything around you might seem a bit surreal. Feelings might include hurt, anger, guilt, shock, uncertainty, and rejection. Emotions will be fluid and won't necessarily come in any order. Sometimes you may need to relive and rethink—again and again—the demise of the relationship, so you can work through it. Sometimes you may need a break from thinking about it at all.

You may spend time second-guessing your actions—"If only I had . . ." or "I should have . . ."—and that can cause anxiety and ambivalence. You will careen from one emotion to the next; just allow them to be as they are, knowing they will change into something else as you go through the grieving process. Healthy grief allows you to experience your feelings in your body, your mind, and your heart.

What's important is to allow yourself to feel what you feel. Don't try to repress or ignore your pain, because it will only come up again later. A mistake many of us make is to try to distract ourselves from painful feelings. It's hard to hurt, but we have to acknowledge and experience our pain. This is an essential part of grief.

Rather than distracting yourself or pushing your feelings away, this is the time to engage in the self-care you need to create a sacred space to process your new grief. This might include the practices described in the Appendix, such as journaling, meditation, guided visualizations, or any of the other ways you cherish and nurture yourself. We can't stress enough how important it is not to deny what you feel; that's why you must also use self-care to give yourself the strength to experience your pain. Your resilience will surprise you.

Denial and bargaining can be especially dangerous traps for relationship junkies. Their whole sense of being is tied up in the relationship and any sign of it ending causes an almost unbearable agony as the fantasy of Prince Charming saving the day begins to fade. Relationship junkies may come up with all sorts of controlling and manipulative behaviors to ward off a break-up—a form of bargaining. They will twist themselves inside out trying to become the exact person they believe their partner wants them to be. They will play helpless, nag, use guilt, jealousy, and a smothering version of caretaking to manipulate and control their partner so they won't leave. They may start to idealize their ex or the relationship, denying the problems that existed. They may convince themselves the break-up was a mistake and that they will be able to convince their ex of that as well. These behaviors are all attempts to deny the reality that the relationship is over and stave off the inevitable grief.

You will certainly experience some depression, and it may be so deep that it's wise to get a psychological evaluation. A professional can help you understand the difference between the natural depression that occurs with any loss and the more severe depression that is about more than this loss alone.

Depression is often a sign of multiple losses that haven't been dealt with. As you grieve, you may dredge up grief for past relationships that have ended but still wound you inside. This is why it's so important to let go and surrender to the experience of grief. Unresolved grief creates an inability to accept the trauma of the loss.

EXERCISE 1. WRITE YOUR EX A LETTER

Writing a letter to someone is a great way to sort through your thoughts and feelings, and putting them on paper is very cathartic. In your letter, you have an opportunity to say everything you have always wanted to say. You can tell your ex how much you long for him/her, miss him/her, and how much he/she hurt you, betrayed you, how bad in bed he/she was, or even how ungrateful he/she is.

You are not going to send the letter. This letter is for you only; it's an opportunity to lay everything out there emotionally so you no longer hold it in your body, your mind, or your heart. Since you're not going to send it, you don't have to watch what you say or how you say it.

After you write it, you can burn the letter in a goodbye ceremony, tear it up, or throw it in the toilet. You can even put it away and reread it whenever you're tempted to try to get back together—to remind yourself of why that relationship will never work.

COLD TURKEY

It is vital that during the grieving process you make no contact with your ex. That includes stopping all forms of communication. Not a text or a phone call or a drive by their house. No leaving voice messages or responding if your ex calls. Not even reading old texts (delete them), checking their Facebook page (unfriend them), or even asking a mutual acquaintance how they are doing.

This period of no contact allows both people in a relationship to break the glue that has been holding them together and detach as a couple. This is the time for each to establish their own autonomy.

Making contact is just a way to avoid the inevitable pain of real ending and grief. You need to create distance from your relationship, so that your mind, body, and spirit can heal. A new door cannot open when you are still holding on to the past.

This is the time to be truthful with yourself and the motivations you have for wanting to see your ex. You may invent reasons to reconnect: You need closure; you need answers to why the relationship failed; you believe you still can be friends. In reality, you don't need any of these things. What you do need is to detach and grieve, and then understand the nature of your addiction, so you don't keep making the same bad choices.

Do not be tempted to try to create a "friends with benefits" relationship after a break-up. That's another fantasy—it *never* works with an ex. You are only avoiding the inevitable, and will become jealous and suspicious if they are dating someone else. "Friends with benefits" is just another term for using each other to avoid the loneliness and disconnection of a break-up.

The only time couples need to be in touch after a break-up is if they are co-parenting. Make those visits brief and, if possible, drop off and pick up the children in public places to avoid going into each other's private space. Limit phone discussions to issues that are solely about the children.

You may still have things at their place or they might have things at yours. If you want your things back, pack up their stuff in a box and mail it to them. Put a note inside asking them to do the same with your stuff. If you don't care about your things, you can discard your ex's belongings after a reasonable amount of time.

Believe me, I (Sherry) know only too well how big a mistake it is to hold on to someone's belongings. I held on to my ex-husband's things for three years after our divorce, afraid to let go, afraid to hurt him by throwing them out—and on some level, clinging to a belief that we were still connected if his things were in my garage. He might call and ask about them; might come by one day to pick them up. In fact, I gave my ex many opportunities to get his things, but he never did. They were really just excuses on my part to get in touch.

All I did was avoid the inevitable pain. Finally, after three years, I reluctantly called a charity group to pick up all his things. It was one of the hardest things I have ever done, and even today, I hold on to some guilt for giving them away.

I do not suggest you wait three years to do what I did. Examine your reasons for holding on to things that belong to your ex. Be honest with yourself about your real intentions, and you will have no choice but to see that you are just making excuses to avoid letting go.

EXERCISE 2. MAKING THE TRANSITION

It's tough to go cold turkey. Here are some ideas for smoothing the transition after a break-up.

- » Make a contract with yourself or with your therapist not to e-mail, text, phone, instant message, or check social media with your ex. Don't go to places that you know they frequent just to make contact.

- » Find supportive friends you can call any time when the urge hits you to reach out to your ex.

- » Join a support group, seek a licensed psychotherapist, join Sex and Love Addicts Anonymous, or find an online group where support is only a call or session away.

- » Engage in self-care. The acronym HALT is a great way to remember all the ways to take care of yourself: Avoid being hungry (H), angry (A), lonely (L), or tired (T).

- » Journal when you get the urge to see your ex. Write about what happened that made you feel that way. Look for patterns and triggers you can avoid.

ACCEPTANCE

Acceptance, the final stage of grief, just means acknowledging things exactly as they are—letting go of all the fantasies and stories, the denial and bargaining. The relationship is over; you and your ex are not getting back together. What's done is done.

Although relationship junkies believe they can control someone else or the outcome of their break-up, the truth is that control is an illusion. What you do have control over is learning how to let go, accept, and surrender the ending of a relationship to a higher power, higher self, a God of your understanding, Buddha, infinite intelligence, the universe, or whoever and whatever you believe in. By letting go and accepting the end of your relationship, you allow the grief process to finally begin so that you can heal. Letting go and accepting the break-up is where true freedom begins and suffering ends. This is where you have the opportunity to rebuild yourself, develop self-esteem, reflect on what you truly want in a new partner and/or your single life. You may reconnect with friends and family you have neglected, appreciate the lessons you have learned, and make peace with the fact that the relationship is over and it's time to get on with your life.

Elizabeth Grace Saunders, the founder and CEO of Real Life, a coaching company, wrote, "I think the most important thing to remember is that even though it can feel excruciatingly painful at times, grief can come to an end. When you grieve well, it gives you a depth and richness nothing else can."

Now is the time to embrace all the lessons you have learned from the break-up. This is the time to create new interests, new perspectives, and new insights into what worked and what didn't. You will feel empowered as you gain some distance from your loss and find meaning from it, but it's not the time to plunge into a new relationship. Rather, think about something you always wanted to do, just for yourself. Maybe it's joining a gym or a book group, taking up yoga, hiking, or knitting. Since you no longer have a partner, you finally have the time to do it.

Sherry took up outrigger paddling after her divorce. It was great exercise (which is also a stress-buster), and she met a whole set of new people to spend time with every week. There was a sense of camaraderie, a feeling of belonging she needed to help her through the grieving process.

Perhaps this is the time to set bigger goals, such as a career change or going back to school. It's also the time to reconnect with the activities and people you neglected while you were in your relationship addiction. Reconnecting will remind you that you are cherished and valued by others. You may not have a love interest at the moment, but you have plenty of people who love you.

EXERCISE 3. HAVE A DINNER PARTY

This is a great way to reconnect with the people you lost touch with when you were so deeply involved with your ex. Think about who you miss and who you'd like to see again; pick two or three people, and invite them to dinner.

It doesn't have to be anything fancy. If the idea of a dinner party seems intimidating, serve take-out food on paper plates, but go shopping for the nice paper plates and get the best take-out food you can. If appropriate, buy a good bottle of wine. Treat yourself and your guests to something special.

Make it a small dinner party, because that's a more personal experience. If you throw a big party, you can end up hiding out in the kitchen or frantically trying to please your guests and actually reconnecting with no one. But when four people sit down around the dinner table, there's conversation, friendship, and connection. Savor those friendships, and let them nourish you.

CHAPTER 6

LETTING GO OF YOUR INNER CHILD

Our adult relationships are reflections of our childhood. When children feel safe and nurtured and secure, they grow up ready to be on their own, full of dignity, confidence, and a sense of their worth. The inner child is all grown up and ready to enter into adult relationships.

But when children learn early on that their needs will not be met or cannot be expressed, they turn to other things for comfort, such as fantasy and escape, as a means to survive and self-soothe. Their childhood is spent feeling unsafe and insecure, and as adults, their inner child still craves the nurturing they missed. They want to create the happy childhood they never had and look for it in adult relationships. The inner child runs the show, often with disastrous results. This is typically the root of relationship addiction. That inner child buys into childhood fantasies of Prince (or Princess) Charming sweeping them off their feet—only to be let down, and in the process, try their hardest to change their partners to make them live up to their illusions. But these efforts are always doomed; no one can rescue your inner child because that is a person in your past.

"The child you once were continues to survive inside your adult shell," Dr. W. Hugh Missildine wrote in *Your Inner Child of the Past.* "Whether we like it or not, we are simultaneously the child we once were who lives in the emotional atmosphere of the past and often interferes in the present, and an adult who tries to forget the past and live wholly in the present.

The child you once were can balk or frustrate your adult satisfactions, embarrass and harass you, make you sick—or enrich your life."

HOLDING ON TO TRAUMA

When we hold on to unresolved pain from childhood, especially trauma and abandonment, these wounds reemerge in adult relationships as toxic shame. We are ashamed to be seen, to be heard, to be known. We are still carrying the shame that originated in our childhood as trauma. Underneath that toxic shame we feel like a fraud, invisible, unlovable, worthless—all aspects of our shame stories that we carry into our adult relationships and the partners we pick.

Toxic shame comes from the messages we received and internalized as children: You aren't good enough, you are undeserving, you need to care for others but others will not care for you. These messages create a false belief system about who we are and what our identity is. Our desperate attempt to please our parents in childhood causes us to split off parts of ourselves and keep those parts hidden.

In his book *Healing the Shame that Binds You*, John Bradshaw wrote, "Shame is internalized when one is abandoned. Abandonment is the precise term to describe how one loses one's authentic self and ceases to exist psychologically." In other words, we reject our very selves. "I won't be selfish, naughty, needy, if only you will love me," an abandoned child begs, and as adults, our inner child is still pleading.

A child never learns how healthy relationships work when early caregivers don't model these relationships. The child learns early on that they are not allowed to express their needs and turns to other comforts, such as fantasizing about being cared for. Fantasizing feels safer than trusting those who were supposed to be loving and nurturing, so the child learns how to manage without a caregiver's love.

Relationship addiction grows from this unhealthy lack of connection and bonding. As a grown-up, the relationship junkie is frantically searching for others to cherish, bond, and connect with them. There is an insatiable, desperate need for affirmation, acceptance, acknowledgment, and a search for unconditional love. The inner child is crying out.

One of my (Sherry's) clients told me about her early childhood trauma and how it led her to search for love in all the wrong places.

"I remember feeling completely responsible for myself from the time I was very young—probably about the age of four when I became ill and almost died from a serious blood disorder. My father was an emotionally unavailable alcoholic. He lived in our home but had little connection with his children. A constant feeling of sadness lingered, and I saw my mother crying or angry most of the time. The trauma of being in a hospital, away from my mother, still affects me today. When I got ill, I felt I had to be a big girl and not cry because I didn't want to burden my already emotionally disturbed mother even more.

"The emotional unavailability and lack of care or respect toward me from my father left me constantly searching for approval and love from the wrong men. And my mother's obsession with controlling my father turned me into a chronic people pleaser. I have spent most of my life seeking approval and validation from her and pretty much anyone I came into contact with. I've molded myself into whatever other people wanted, hundreds, perhaps thousands, of times. Only now, at forty-one years old, am I starting to be true to myself. Subsequently, I have never had a healthy romantic relationship, mostly because I don't know what that is."

In this chapter, we're going to use the word "parents" to talk about the people who failed you as a child. But it could have been anyone in a caretaker role—a relative, a teacher, a babysitter, or someone else who caused your trauma. As you read this chapter, understand the word "parent" to mean whoever made you feel unsafe and un-nurtured as a child.

OWNING YOUR TRUTH

One of the consequences of shame is that it causes us to deny the truth. We hide away the shameful pain of our past, and we can never heal wounds that we won't even admit are there.

Healing childhood trauma starts with moving from denial to acknowledgment. It is important to identify neglect, abuse, any fracture in early attachment, where the trauma occurred, and who was involved. These are painful, scary things that have been buried deep, and you should not dig them up alone. Some safe places to share the experiences of childhood trauma are support groups, 12-step groups such as Sex and Love Addicts Anonymous (SLAA) meetings, a spiritual advisor, or a trusted friend. By talking to others in a safe environment, you are bringing the light to that which is dark. Allowing the unconscious to become conscious is the first step in healing.

You'll also need to find a qualified psychotherapist who understands trauma and uses modalities that specifically help heal early childhood trauma wounds. Some of those modalities include prolonged exposure therapy, trauma-focused cognitive behavioral therapy, somatic experiencing, cognitive processing trauma, eye movement desensitization and reprocessing (EMDR), and psychodrama. Other modalities are constantly being developed to deal with the after-effects of trauma. Find a therapist and a modality that resonates with you; the same therapy is not right for every person.

As you will recall from the Introduction, both of us (Beth and Sherry) saw therapists to help us acknowledge and deal with our childhood trauma. These therapeutic experiences were life-changing for both of us. Beth saw a more traditional talk therapist, while Sherry chose somatic experiencing.

I (Sherry) found that although my mind didn't remember some of the experiences of my early childhood trauma, my body did. What our heads forget, our bodies often remember. Somatic experiencing was developed by Dr. Peter A. Levine specifically to address the effects of trauma. He observed that although animals are routinely under threat in the wild, they don't suffer from the effects of chronic stress the way humans do. This is because they are able to physically release the energy they accumulate during fight-or-flight reactions to stressful events. Humans, though, often miss out on discharging this stressful energy because shame, judgment, and fear block our natural ways of regulating the nervous system. However, in order to heal, emotions must be felt and brought out into the open rather than being hidden in the body. Somatic experiencing aims to help people process a traumatic event by moving past this stage where they are stuck. By getting old negative energy out of the body, they not only get unstuck, but they also make room for positive experiences.

The process of learning how to ground myself and becoming aware of the bodily sensations related to the past trauma is how I processed my old childhood wounds. By alternating between the sensations associated with trauma and accessing soothing sources of strength and comfort, I was able to discharge the old trauma stuck in my body. The most important aspect of somatic experiencing was learning how to self-regulate my emotions. This has allowed me to stay present in my body without having to run to something outside myself to be soothed.

I realized that for too many years, a new relationship was the only soothing solution I had to overcome the trauma I felt in my body. Now that I have released all that negative energy, the discomfort of anxiety, chronic feelings of emptiness, fear of abandonment, and chronic loneliness has been released. Having a psychotherapist who specializes in trauma treatment has given me a safe environment to do this sacred work.

ACCEPTING YOUR PAST

The next step in healing early trauma is acceptance. Acceptance means understanding that the trauma occurred and there was nothing you could have done to prevent it. It's letting go of the "what if's" and "if only's."

You cannot change your past, no matter how much you might want to, and you cannot recreate your past in the present. Acceptance means understanding this not just in your brain, but in your heart.

Coming to a place of acceptance is no easy task, and, again, a psychotherapist can help. Why would you even want to accept the trauma of your past? One of Sherry's clients explained quite eloquently what happened for her when she had a therapy breakthrough about acceptance.

"In recovery circles we hear about acceptance being the first port of call to get well. I thought it was the most horrendous concept I'd ever heard. How was I going to accept the years of crap I'd endured from others, and from myself? There was too much injustice. Nobody was taking responsibility for their part in my demise. I was angry—for decades. And I had a right to be. But was this how I was going to live my life until my time was up—angry, resentful, and full of hate? And then I heard that acceptance does not mean approval. It's simply taking responsibility for the condition of my life right now. And it is handing back the pain and torture other people inflicted on me and placing it at their feet. It's refusing to remain victimized, and the essence of self-empowerment. From the point of complete acceptance, I was able to make choices about how I lived my life instead of giving my power away. The choice to accept and let go has been the most important, but painful, part of my recovery."

EXERCISE 1. JOURNALING

Writing in a journal promotes self-awareness and clarity. Putting your feelings on paper takes them out of your mind, which clears up the clutter and inner conflict that childhood trauma brings. You also have an opportunity to engage more of your senses, so you can find the transformation you are seeking. (To learn more about journaling and how to get the most out of it, see the Appendix.)

Start by writing down the emotions and physical sensations that come to the surface when you reflect on childhood trauma. These might include rage, anxiety, fear, depression, and shock. Write down the name of each emotion: "I feel _____." This will help you cut through the tangle of feelings, sort through each one, and, eventually, lay it to rest.

When you have your list of emotions, sit in a quiet place and examine each one individually.

» Notice how the emotion feels in your body—the physical sensation.

» Acknowledge how the emotion has affected you.

» Get curious about the emotion. Be the witness or observer of your emotion; watch it go by rather than being stuck in it.

» Express the emotion to your inner self.

» Own the emotion by taking responsibility for it, without blaming your negative emotion on others.

» Share the emotion with a trusted friend or in a support group.

» Let go of the emotion. This does not mean you are pushing away or repressing your emotion. You accept your emotion with understanding but distance yourself from it. You are no longer allowing this emotion to overwhelm or engulf you. An emotion is part of you but does not define you; you are not your emotion.

» Acknowledge the process. Otherwise you may bury the emotion away, rationalizing painful betrayals from your past. If you don't acknowledge your emotions and the process of letting go of them, you may begin acting out old wounds in inappropriate ways. Acknowledging and working through feelings is not a sign of weakness, but rather is a way to no longer have to carry the baggage of that painful emotion.

» Send out forgiveness and compassion to yourself and to those who have caused these emotions.

FORGIVENESS AND COMPASSION

Did that last point in the journaling exercise about forgiveness seem almost impossible to you? Forgiveness can be very difficult, even too much to bear for many people, because forgiving someone for a terrible hurt seems like letting them off the hook, saying it was okay or that now you don't mind that this painful thing happened. That's not at all what we mean by forgiveness.

Sometimes we get hung up on words, so we're going to suggest that if forgiveness seems like letting someone off the hook, instead try thinking about forgiveness as simply letting go of the hurt. Forgiveness is for you, so you can stop hurting. It has very little to do with the person who hurt you. Oprah Winfrey once wrote, "Forgiveness is giving up the hope that the past could have been any different."

Imagine all your anger and pain is a burning hot coal that you want to throw at the person who hurt you. You carry it around with you everywhere, hold it tight in your hand, ready for that moment when you will be able to hurl it at that person and hurt them the way they hurt you.

The problem is that as you carry it, that hot coal is burning your hand, causing you more pain every day. Your pain will never stop, your hand will never heal, until you put that burning coal down. That's all forgiveness is: putting down the terrible pain and anger you carry—no matter how righteous, no matter how justified—so that it does not continue to burn you up.

Forgiveness allows you to release those negative emotions and return to a natural state of joy and love in the present. In her book *A Return to Love*, spiritual teacher Marianne Williamson wrote, "Healing occurs in the present, not the past. We are not held back by the love we didn't receive in the past, but by the love we're not extending in the present." When you have so much pain associated with your past, forgiveness is very hard. But for your own healing, you need to do it.

EXERCISE 2. MINDFULNESS

Psychologists have found that we can actually change the way we think about things just by becoming aware of our thought patterns and consciously redirecting them. (To learn more about mindfulness, see the Appendix.) When you catch yourself feeling angry or abandoned or when you feel your inner child acting like a hungry ghost, tell yourself, "I've let go of that anger. I'm not that person anymore."

It feels almost too simple, doesn't it? But research has shown that reframing and redirecting our thoughts is actually very effective in changing our thought patterns.

This can also be part of a larger strategy, called acting "as if." You think about the person you want to become and act as if you already are that person. In the beginning, you'll feel like you're faking it—acting as if you are secure and confident and have let go of the inner child that was traumatized. But eventually, your mind and body learn the habits of your "as if" persona, and it becomes your true self. It really does work!

OUR PARENTS ARE JUST FLAWED PEOPLE

Because parents have so much power over their children, they become larger-than-life figures. We depend on them for our very survival—both physical and emotional. Long after we have become adults and can take care of ourselves—sometimes even long after our parents are dead—they continue to have outsized roles in our lives.

If you suffered a childhood trauma, your parents may be the monsters who never gave you what you needed, who abused you, who made you feel shameful and less than. But in fact, your parents are just flawed people—and most likely, people with their own childhood trauma. Remember, we learn about relationships from our parents, and that includes parenting relationships. Our parents learned parenting from their parents. So chances are they were unnurtured as well. They didn't know how to nurture you because no one nurtured them.

One of the hardest things to do as an adult is to stop seeing our parents as larger-than-life figures, as caretakers who failed us, and instead to just see them as ordinary people. Most adults are never actually able to do this. They are never able to let go of the mirror of the past and see their parents clearly, in the present. Without this crucial step, you will never be able to feel compassion for them. And without compassion, you will never be able to let go of the pain and anger that is weighing you down, that is burning you up every day.

If your parents are still alive, when you interact with them, try to be in the moment; react to what they are actually saying and doing *right then*, rather than falling into old patterns of action and reaction, anger and resentment. If they say things that hurt you, back away and protect yourself, rather than lashing out. Ask them about their own childhoods: What was their life like? How did their parents or grandparents treat them? As you learn about their lives, you may begin to see some familiar patterns from your own life.

As I (Sherry) mentioned earlier, when I look at my own family history, there are patterns that have repeated themselves. My grandmother, my mother, and I did not receive the nurturing we clearly needed, leaving us vulnerable to picking unavailable partners. As you look back at your own family background, what patterns are you repeating?

If your parents are no longer alive, you may still want to understand what patterns have led you to the choices you have made or are still making. Or perhaps you are trying to replace what you have lost because your parents are no longer here. I know when my own father died, I really missed the security he had always provided me, even as a grown woman. He was my rock, and when he died, I felt the earth beneath me crumble. As my dad was dying, I lost my fifteen-year-old dog as well. It made me extremely vulnerable to choosing partners out of neediness and grief.

As I look back, I see the choices I made came from desperation. Be mindful of the choices you are making in your own life. Are your choices coming from a place of empowerment, or are you making choices to make up for what you have lost?

EXERCISE 3. YOU KNOW YOU'VE LET GO WHEN . . .

Learning to let go of the emotions associated with childhood trauma is the last step in letting go of your inner child. You finally leave behind the heaviness of this past pain, so you can move on and live happy, joyful, and free.

You will know you have let go of the past when you honestly say that all the following are true.

» You see yourself and your parents as equals.

» You have more compassion for where your parents came from and understand that they are products of their environment.

» You are able to share memories of childhood wounds with someone you trust.

» You allow yourself to feel and release the negative emotions that arise from early childhood wounds.

» You understand that although you may experience feelings from past pain, you do not have to act on them. Instead, you can act "as if" you have moved on.

» Except for the purpose of bringing old wounds into the light to be healed, you are learning to live in the moment.

EXERCISE 4. POSITIVE AFFIRMATIONS

Positive affirmations are declarations or mantras that you repeat to help you reprogram your subconscious mind so you can achieve a new goal. (See the Appendix to learn more about positive affirmations.)

Repeat this affirmation twice a day as a way to release childhood pain and trauma.

I accept that my parents did the best they could for me.

I forgive them for any wrongdoing they were unaware of.

I also forgive myself for holding any resentments against them.

As I learn to forgive myself, I am able to forgive others more freely.

BECOMING YOUR OWN PARENT

We might long for a partner to parent our inner child the way we were never parented, but healthy relationships between adults are not about parenting. They are partnerships between equals. As long as we yearn for parents rather than true partners, we will never break free from our addiction and enter into satisfying relationships.

The inner child is like a wounded, hungry little ghost, haunting us with demands for parenting. The way out is by becoming your own nurturing parent to your inner child. The more you love your inner child, the less you will need the validation of others to feel whole, and the less you'll need to look to others for safety and security. You have the ability to nurture the fearful child within you. Re-parenting your inner child lets you know you are lovable and worthy. It gives you permission to accept the totality of yourself—even the parts you have hidden away.

EXERCISE 5. NURTURE YOUR INNER CHILD

Find a photograph of yourself as a small child. If you don't have one, imagine yourself as the innocent child you were. Know that this little child exists within you, with all their tender feelings, thoughts, and beliefs. If you have neglected them, let them know how sorry you are. Imagine yourself talking to that child now, as an adult. Ask your inner child to tell you what has made them feel unsafe and frightened. Let them speak freely and openly. Listen carefully.

Now, allow the nurturing adult you are to give your inner child the reassurance they so desperately need. Let your inner child know how much they are loved, how safe they are with you. Let them know you will care for them and that you will never hurt or leave them.

EXERCISE 6. INNER CHILD MEDITATION

We're honored that Missy Kozel, a client of Sherry's, wrote this guided meditation just for this book. (We're sharing it with her permission.) Listening to a guided meditation can lead you on a psycho-spiritual path to calm and healing. (To learn more about guided meditation, see the Appendix.)

You can record yourself reading this guided meditation, or ask a friend who has a calming voice to record it for you, and then play it back as often as you'd like. Lie or sit down in a quiet room to listen to this guided meditation, and make sure you will not be disturbed. Now begin.

Find a comfortable position, close your eyes, and try to relax.

Take a deep breath in through your nose and out through your mouth. Feel the air going in and out of your body, and notice how it feels. Keep breathing and feel your breaths.

As you listen to my voice, a path opens up in front of you. Follow it as I count back from five . . . four . . . three . . . two . . . one. As you walk, there is a light that grows brighter and brighter at the end of your path. When you come to the light, put your hands up and feel its warmth radiating outward. Take a step through the light, and find yourself standing in front of your first childhood home.

Look at your old house and notice the many details you might have forgotten over time. As you look, the door opens, and an excited child bounds out. You recognize this child as you when you were younger. Take in the condition of your inner child, and look at the expression on his/her face. Kneel down, so you are face to face.

Introduce yourself to your inner child, and give him/her a hug. Tell him/her that you have lived the same life and you understand the pain that he/she has been through. Allow your inner child to grieve with you, and comfort her/

him as he/she needs it. Allow him/her to feel his/her pain and let it go. When he/she is ready, dry your inner child's tears and tell him/her that he/she is loved and worthy, until you see him/her begin to understand.

Now, take your inner child's hand, and begin walking down the street. You wave goodbye to your mother and father and make your way together down the road, by blooming flowers and chirping birds. The next time you look at your inner child, you see him/her start to fade, as he/she tells you, "We are one," and you feel his/her energy combine with yours.

You continue walking down the road until you see a lovely garden with a bench that seems to be calling to you. You sit, letting the sun and breeze play against your skin. Soak it in. You hear the breeze blow through, and it has a message for you from your higher power: "I love you, and I am sorry that you have felt such pain. Everything is going to be okay. You are amazing, and I love you unconditionally."

Feel these words in the breeze and the sun on your skin, and take them in. Relax on the bench and continue to focus on your breathing. When you are ready, begin to come back into yourself, one body part at a time, taking all of the love from your inner child and your higher power with you.

CHAPTER 7

SOMETHING TO BELIEVE IN

One of the hallmarks of relationship junkies is that they are always trying to create a "perfect" relationship—to bring to life their fantasy of what that looks like. Perfectionism is actually a compulsion to control, which is why relationship addicts sometimes feel like controlling partners. When everything seems precarious and desperate, control creates the illusion of stability and reliability.

What if you didn't have to control everything? What if you could just worry about what you do and let someone or something else take care of the rest? The opposite of perfectionism is faith, and faith is surrendering your efforts and your life to a higher power.

Surrendering to a higher power is an integral part of just about every addiction recovery program, and it may be the most controversial. Not everyone believes in a higher power, and not everyone agrees with the idea of surrender. But we believe surrendering to whatever your higher power is—god or goddess, the universe, the force, your intuition—is crucial for recovery, because surrender teaches us what we can and can't control and what we should and should not trust.

When I (Beth) was a kid, my grandmother taught everyone in our family how to swim. We started off by learning how to float on our back. Nana would take us into the shallow water and place two hands under our back while we floated. You can't float when you're all tensed up, so the key was learning how to relax. "Just let go and lie back," Nana would say. "I won't let you go under the water." And because we loved and trusted Nana, we did. When we had the feeling of floating, she'd take one hand away. "See how you're still okay," she'd point out. "When you relax, it gets easier." Then, when we were sufficiently relaxed, she'd take the other hand away. "You're floating! You can do it!"

Holding you up is a property of water. If you just relax and trust it to do its thing, the water will hold you up every time. The only time it doesn't hold you up is when you tense up, fight against it, and try to control everything. That's what it means to surrender to a higher power. The universe, life, will hold you up, but only if you let it.

Surrendering to a higher power means you can relax, you can trust. When you try to control everything, you are closed off to all of life's possibilities. When you surrender to a higher power, you are open to whatever might come along—including things you haven't thought of and can't even imagine.

THE LAW OF ATTRACTION

In our previous book, *Infinite Recovery*, we talked about the Law of Attraction and how it can be a powerful tool to help people overcome substance addictions. It can be just as powerful when you're faced with relationship addiction.

The Law of Attraction says that the thoughts and emotions we put out into the universe shape our reality. Thoughts and emotions are a form of energy, and the energy we project into the world is the same energy we will attract back to us. Whether you are focusing on what you want in your life or what you don't want, whatever you direct your attention to is what will come about. As we said in that book, "It's important to be very clear in your own mind about what it is you desire and want to manifest in your life, because the universe is listening."

If you spend your time thinking about how you are unfulfilled, angry, and anxious, you will attract those feelings back to yourself. If you are emanating contentment and confidence, that is what you will attract back. We create our reality by the statements we make and the intentions we put forth to the universe.

The proponents of the Law of Attraction say universal vibrations power the attraction: All forms of matter and energy (including mental energy) vibrate, and energy is drawn to other energy that is vibrating on the same wavelength. As we become aware of the thoughts and energy we are sending out, we can change our vibration by thinking in ways that are more in harmony with what we really want. But you don't need to believe in the concept of a vibrating universe to make the Law of Attraction work for you.

Psychologists know that people with a positive outlook have happier, healthier, more socially engaged lives, while people who are trapped in negative ways of thinking tend to be unhappy and isolated. So if you keep telling yourself that you are empty, unloved, and desperate, you will be. If you let your angry, wounded inner child tell you that you will always be alone, you will be. And if you tell yourself that you are okay alone, you will be. You can change the way you think about yourself and the world, and surrendering to a higher power—learning to relax and trust the universe—is a big part of that.

The Law of Attraction also influences the kind of people you attract. When you are in a grasping state, desperate to have someone to fill the emptiness inside, you attract others with similar unhealthy behaviors. As you create wholeness within, you become more available for someone who is also whole and healthy to show up in your life. What you put out into the universe is exactly what you will receive. You create the reality you live in, so feeling comfortable with yourself allows the universe to bring you exactly what you desire.

Ask yourself, when did you lose trust in the universe that you wouldn't receive the relationship and life you desire? Are you ready to treat yourself with the love and respect you deserve? Declare to the universe that you will be honest with yourself, relax, and trust your higher power.

EXERCISE 1. JOURNALING

To understand what kind of energy you are sending out—and what kind you are attracting—it's important to take stock. Here are some questions to ask yourself. Write the first one down on the top of a piece of paper, and then write down whatever answers come to mind. Each question builds on the one before, so when you have answered one as fully as you think you can, move on to the next question.

» What stories do I tell myself about relationships?
» Where did these stories come from?
» Am I willing to change the stories?
» What is it that I really desire?
» Why haven't I received it yet?
» Am I resisting a relationship by blocking the good from coming into my life?
» Am I getting anything out of blocking the good?
» If I stopped blocking the good, what would my life look like?
» Am I doing anything to move my life forward?
» Can I change my thoughts so my life can change?

YOUR DIVINE SELF

Rather than having a healthy relationship with the divine, relationship junkies let their partner become their higher power. We are perpetrators of our own misery and suffering when we believe someone else is responsible for our well-being. It is painful when we finally wake up and see our partners for who they really are and realize it was us who chose to believe in fairytales. A much greater source of well-being awaits when we trust in a true higher power.

When we finally realize we are in control only of the intimacy we have within ourselves, we will get what we need. In our obsessions over our love objects, we believe we can control all the outcomes in our relationships—but we only find ourselves frustrated and mostly out of control. It is a higher power that will lead us to peace, not Mr. or Ms. Right.

There is an infinite source of strength we can access from our higher power. We can let go of the struggle to relive our past and reshape our present by connecting to that source. It's time to get out of a "don't have" mentality—"I don't have what I need/want"—and believe the universe is going to bring us exactly the right partner at exactly the right time, when we are truly ready to receive.

Ways to connect to a higher power can include prayer, meditation, guided visualizations, positive affirmations, forgiveness, gratitude, and reading spiritual literature. Spirituality can also be found in 12-step meetings, church, synagogue, temple, mosque, and/or creating your own sacred space in your home. Do not confuse spirituality with religion. Spirituality is your personal relationship with your own higher power. It is as close to organized religion—or as far away—as you want it to be. You just need to be willing and open to that relationship. As Beth's Nana said, relax and trust.

Some see their higher power as something that lives outside them, and others view their higher power as a wiser source that lies within. Spirituality is where mind, body, and spirit come together as one in perfect harmony—and that can be anywhere.

If the idea of having a higher power at first feels uncomfortable or if you have a hard time really believing there is a power out there that is working for you, try acting as if there is one. Just pretend. Remember, the energy we send out into the world is the same energy we will receive. Act as if your higher power is nurturing you. Acting "as if" is a powerful choice all by itself, and opens up all sorts of possibilities—including a spiritual awakening. There is nothing more empowering than surrendering the emptiness you might be feeling inside not to another unhealthy relationship, but instead to your divine self. Your higher power will embody the unconditional love and acceptance you have been so desperately seeking.

EXERCISE 2. POSITIVE AFFIRMATIONS

Acting as if your higher power is looking out for you, even when you don't quite believe it, is a powerful way to coax your mind and emotions to open up to the possibility. Affirmations—positive statements you make—will help you transform "as if" into your reality. Here are some positive affirmations for surrendering to your higher power.

I act in accordance with my higher power.

I am aligned with my higher self.

I do what my higher power guides me to do.

When I make contact with the higher power within me, all is possible.

All the energies of the universe direct me to my greatest good.

Connection with my higher power brings me peace and joy.

Divine guidance is always available to me.

Deep in my core lies the infinite wisdom of the universe.

GETTING WHAT YOU NEED

If you are tired of being single and of the disappointments of dating, we get it more than you can imagine. When you give up the dating cycle and surrender to a higher power, you actually gain more control over what seems uncontrollable—finding the right mate. By turning your fears and doubts over to your higher power, you make space for the universe to bring you exactly what you need and want. You are allowing love to come to you, rather than frantically searching for it.

A client we'll call Kate came to see Sherry about panic attacks that were keeping her awake at night. She was in a new relationship with John, and from the beginning, she was afraid of losing him even though there were no signs the relationship was in trouble. However, she became obsessed with making John love her and ultimately marry her.

When Kate was growing up, her parents taught her that real happiness comes from being married and having children. Before she met John, she had a fulfilling single life, but she could not shake that nagging pressure that she should be married. Messages from her parents that single women were "less than" were at the bottom of her anxiety attacks.

Her obsessions over John drove her to stalking behavior. She would drive by his house to make sure he was not out with someone else. She watched him incessantly, and if he changed a date or was late, she assumed he must not love her or wanted to break up. She always thought about the worst-case scenario, filling her world and his with negativity and doubt. Eventually, her behaviors sabotaged the relationship and John began to pull back. He told her he still wanted to be in the relationship, but needed more time away from her and more space for himself.

Kate agreed to this without question because she couldn't imagine not being with John. But putting his needs before her own is also a kind of neediness. Our work together was reframing her beliefs that she was nothing without John. She had to learn to ask for what she needed in the relationship without insecurity or fear that he might reject her. The goal was to help her let go of her extreme attachment to John, even if that meant losing the relationship.

Kate started to engage in activities she enjoyed, without John. She let her family know they no longer would be allowed to pressure her into marriage. She was learning to release the fear of being rejected, the fear that the relationship might not work, and the fear that she might have to face life alone. She stopped looking for signs that John didn't love her or wanted to leave her and accepted his behaviors at face value. She stopped trying to control the future of the relationship and began enjoying it in the present. She stopped obsessing over John's every move and put the focus back on her own life and what made her happy. She began to trust her higher power to make things come out right—whatever "right" might end up being.

When she did this, Kate started feeling more in balance and in alignment with her true desires. Her self-esteem improved, as she stopped trying to please John in how she dressed, what she ate, what activities they shared, and who they hung out with. She stopped feeling resentful about trying to be someone she believed he wanted, rather than being true to herself. She realized she had abandoned her dignity, which had left her feeling empty and desperate.

Once she let go of this desperation, John began to appreciate her more. She stopped living in fear and began living with self-respect and autonomy. She stopped obsessing over John and trusted him, and was surprised to find that their relationship improved tremendously. What Kate learned is that when you surrender to your higher power, rather than to a relationship, the universe conspires on your behalf and your desires will be made manifest.

Whatever you focus your attention on is what will be manifested in your life. This is the time to change your mindset from uncertainty to trust, from fear to belief, and from skepticism to faith that what you desire will come to you. Start envisioning in your core that a healthy relationship is on its way.

LISTENING TO YOUR HIGHER POWER

If you're a relationship junkie, you've made some poor decisions for yourself in the past. If you are questioning the relationship you're in, making contact with your higher power can assist you in your confusion and guide you toward the best decision you can make for yourself. Ask your higher power what is in your best interest and listen for the answer in meditation.

Letting go is where real freedom exists, when we come to understand we no longer need to make decisions on our own. Having a higher power to rely on brings us in contact with a spiritual essence that is there to guide us.

When you know you have the assistance of your higher power by your side, you realize you no longer have to push upstream to make a relationship work or to make yourself or your partner perfect. It's a relief when you realize you are powerless over someone else's behavior and the fantasy images you have projected onto your partners. You no longer need to manipulate others to be what you want them to be—or manipulate yourself to be what others want you to be. There is no more needing to fix your relationship because you can just accept that what doesn't work can't be fixed. Your higher power is telling you it's time to move on, and it will give you the strength to listen and act.

When you were stuck in your relationship addiction, you made your significant other your higher power, and when things didn't work out as you hoped, you were usually left feeling rejected or abandoned. Now, with a real higher power, you can connect to the truest version of yourself with or without a partner. Knowing there is a sacred voice within, you can trust you are on the right path.

I remember two weeks before I (Sherry) was to marry husband number three, when my higher power tried to steer me down the right path and I would not listen. I was thirty-six, and my biological clock was ticking away. I had a wedding planned with three hundred guests, and yet, something deep in my core was gnawing at me. Husband number three was verbally abusive to my daughter and to me. Although it was undiagnosed, I believe he had obsessive compulsive disorder, which is characterized by unreasonable thoughts and fears (obsessions) that lead you to perform repetitive behaviors (compulsions). His disorder made him very critical of my behavior—even the smallest things. When I cooked, if there was any grease left anywhere in the kitchen, he yelled at me. If my daughter ate more than he thought she needed, he criticized my parenting. When I didn't do exactly what he demanded, he got angry and yelled or sulked and would not talk to me for days. If I kept quiet and did what he said, I would just receive more criticism for not doing it correctly.

I knew in my heart I should cancel the wedding. Unfortunately, not having a relationship with a higher power, as I do today, I married him anyway. I didn't listen to that warning voice deep inside me. I will never forget that just before I walked down the aisle, a pedestal of flowers fell on my dress. I knew that was a sign from my higher power that I was making a huge mistake. While I could hear the voice of my higher power, I had not yet surrendered to it.

As I knew it would, my third husband's criticism and verbal abuse just got worse. After four months, I found myself packing up two garbage bags full of my and my daughter's clothes and could not get out of that house, and that marriage, fast enough.

When I look back at most of my marriages, there were always signs, but I ignored them. My need to fill up my empty soul and my lack of trust that the universe would give me exactly what I need were always greater than any wisdom I might receive from my higher power.

If you are rushing into a relationship knowing it could be a mistake, if you are afraid you won't find someone else to love you, that is not a good enough reason to partner with the wrong person. The universe is there to hold you up, and it will—if you can just walk through the loneliness, knowing your higher power is looking out for you.

EXERCISE 3. PRAYER

You may never have prayed before, or you may have prayed when you were a child in a way that was guided by your family or a religious institution. That kind of "institutional" prayer is not what we mean. Prayer just means opening yourself to your higher power and honoring whatever you feel in response.

If you believe in a divinity, perhaps that response is a direct message. If you believe in the Law of Attraction, perhaps that response is positive energy. If you do not believe in the divine, perhaps the response is your own wise intuition, guiding you on the right path.

Set aside a quiet time in a sacred space—someplace you feel calm and safe and unhurried. This is a place where you can connect with your higher power and the divinity that lies within you. If you are someone who believes in the Law of Attraction, this is a space to get in touch with the energy of your thoughts.

You might set up a sacred space in your home where you place objects that have a spiritual meaning for you, such as crystals, incense, or other symbols that resonate with your belief system. Your sacred space might also be outdoors, either in your garden or simply walking in a park and observing the nature that surrounds you.

To reach inside to your intuition, you need to put aside your ego. There is a great acronym in 12-step programs, that EGO stands for Edging God Out. This is how your ego gets in the way of your conscious contact with your higher power. Taking the time to pray or speak to your higher power or higher self opens up the pathway, establishing a soul connection with the divine, the place where intuition lives.

We love this quote from Dr. Wayne Dyer, the psychologist and teacher, which describes the process of prayer and intuition: "If prayer is you talking to God, then intuition is God talking back." Knowing and trusting that the universe always responds is the first step in trusting your higher power. You just need to ask, and then learn how to listen.

Intuition can show up as a sudden thought, a dream, or that gut feeling in your core. This is your higher power speaking to you, and this is where your answers can be found. We all have intuition, but sometimes we allow our fears to take over and drown it out. Begin listening, praying, and paying attention to what your higher power is whispering to you.

CHAPTER 8

YOU DON T COMPLETE ME: LEARNING TO LIVE FABULOUSLY ON YOUR OWN

Everybody knows that line from the movie *Jerry Maguire*: "You complete me." That sentence embodies the ultimate relationship junkie fantasy: You're an incomplete person living an incomplete life, and only a relationship will make you complete. That's a dangerous idea and one we'd like you to let go of once and for all.

The truth is only *you* can complete you. Believing someone else can complete you chips away at your dignity and your self-worth. It's belittling, to say the least. Needing someone else to make you feel whole means admitting that you can't take care of your own needs, wants, and desires. It says, "I can't be alone at any cost. I am not enough. I can't cope with life without a partner."

But you can; everything you need in your heart is already inside you. You know how to nurture yourself—you've been doing it for years. Loving yourself with deep compassion and forgiveness can complete any missing parts you long for. Everything you need in your life, you can get. You don't need to get it all from one person, but you can get a little from a lot of people, and it will all add up to what you need.

As we've already seen, we create our realities by the statements we make and the intentions we put forth. There is a lot of negativity in the statement, "You complete me."

It's far more positive and more empowering to say, "The right partner would add to my life but doesn't sustain it." You're already whole, with or without a partner.

You are creating your own misery and suffering when you believe someone else is responsible for your well-being. Like so many other false beliefs we have explored in this book, you are setting yourself up for failure and disappointment. Ask yourself:

» When did you start believing that only a partner can complete you? What did you gain by believing this lie? What did you lose?

» What is missing inside of you that makes you feel you are not enough and must have a partner to complete you?

» What would happen if you were on your own? Would you then be half a person?

» How would you feel if *you* completed you?

One of my (Sherry's) clients told me exactly how it feels to complete yourself. "I never thought it was possible to be happy without a romantic relationship. At one point any relationship would do, as long as I was in one. Even if it was a sick relationship, I'd rather complain about it than leave it behind. Relationships defined who I was and fed my meager self-worth. If a man wanted me, surely it meant I was worth something.

"Through years of work, I am now at a point where my value is based on the care I give myself. I became my own biggest fan, my own nurturer, my own lover, and my own inner parent. I build a life for myself and my children independently, and while I very much want to have a relationship in my life, I will not settle for just anyone or any type of treatment. I value myself highly. I look in the mirror and see a beautiful, strong, intelligent, compassionate woman who deserves the best kind of relationship and the best kind of treatment from myself and everyone around me."

EXERCISE 1. POSITIVE AFFIRMATIONS

It's important to start this new phase of your life—the one where you feel comfortable being on your own—with lots of positive energy and intentions. It's time to declare to yourself and to the universe that you know who you are, what you need, and how to get it. Try these positive affirmations.

I have banished my fantasies once and for all about a partner completing me.

I am ready to embrace the possibility of being alone.

I am a powerful person on my own, no matter what family, friends, or society say about being without a partner.

I deserve a healthy relationship filled with intimacy and respect, and will not settle for less.

I will continue to be honest with myself, no matter what the consequences.

WHAT'S SO GREAT ABOUT BEING ON YOUR OWN?

Being on your own frees you to explore yourself and your life in a way you simply cannot if you have a partner. This applies to the biggest things—and the smallest. Feel like having nothing but salad and mashed potatoes for dinner? You can, because you're not making dinner for anyone but yourself. Ever thought about going vegan or Paleo or gluten-free? Now you can try it. Change the curtains, change your wardrobe, change the color of your bathroom—you don't have to consider anyone's opinions but your own. Want a cat/dog/fish/parakeet? Want to convert half your living room into a yoga space? Want to spend your Saturdays volunteering at a youth center—or being pampered at a spa? You don't have to worry about what your partner wants anymore. What do *you* want?

As for the big things, think about a career change or going back to school. When you were living your life for someone else, would you contemplate the time and commitment of taking a class, even just for fun? Now that your time is your own, it's possible. It's also possible to think about taking a job in another city or even another country. You can do what's best for *you*. Your choices are yours and yours alone.

Being on your own means you have the freedom and the space to explore who you really are and to become your authentic self. You've probably spent a lifetime trying to be who your parents, your teachers, your lovers, your partners wanted you to be. You've twisted yourself to suit them because you were so afraid of rejection. But when rejection no longer has that power over you—when you're ready to be on your own— there's no need to be anyone but yourself. Do you remember what that looks and feels like?

A client told Sherry, "After some years in recovery, a new realization dawned on me. I had spent my entire life reinventing myself according to what other people wanted me to be. There's a generic set of rules that's supposed to apply to everyone, and realistically that doesn't work. As a woman, I discovered that practically every adversity I encountered in my life was because someone was trying to control my femininity and put me in a box I most certainly didn't fit into. The conflict inside me between my true self and the expectations of society was torture. I had to find out who I was, and in the process discovered that much of my trouble came from a damaged, screwed-up idea about what it meant to be a woman.

"Redefining what it means to be feminine has revolutionized my entire life, especially concerning my sexual life and relationships with men. I had to explore all the ways in which my femininity was damaged and exploited and then repair it. Now, as a whole person and a powerful woman, I have true freedom to be and express who I am on every level."

If you have children, you get to raise them with your own values, based on what resonates for you, not your partner. I (Sherry) spent years trying to fill the empty seat at my kitchen table with a "father" for my daughter, after her biological father left when she was one year old. I spent endless amounts of energy on endless relationships, trying to fit square pegs into a round hole. These men (who had never had children but somehow thought they knew all about child-rearing) would sweep in and try to control how I should be raising my sweet little girl. I actually was forced to divorce two of them due to their unrealistic expectations of what they believed a "good mother" should be—and for that matter, how a "good child" should behave.

What freedom we found when I was finally on my own with my daughter and able to guide her in whatever way I saw fit for our little family! We went to single parent camp every Memorial Day weekend for years, we went on Club Med vacations, we ate out when and where we wanted, and created a mother-daughter connection that is indescribable—one I certainly never had with my own mother. There is a special bond that exists between a single parent and their children that a traditional family can't provide, or even understand. I am so grateful for the special relationship I have with my daughter and wouldn't change one thing. I am a single grandmother, too (although I have a boyfriend at the moment), and I get to create an incredible connection with my granddaughter as well.

EXERCISE 2. JOURNALING

It's important to be aware of all the things you have been denying yourself because you were focusing on your partner. Figure out what you've been giving up, so you'll know what you can give yourself now. Start your journal by writing down all the things you haven't done because you thought your partner wouldn't enjoy them: romantic movies, Thai food, bicycling, having a cat, visiting your family—whatever those things are. Think of all the things you've been missing out on and denying yourself.

Now, make that your to-do list. Write each item at the top of a blank page. As you do each thing, write on that page how it makes you feel. Note your physical and your emotional reactions. Do you feel relieved, giddy, light, joyful? Embrace the experience, whatever it is.

EVERY SINGLE DETAIL

Yes, there are a lot of details about single life that can be difficult to navigate. There's always more than one way around these kinds of details, including a solution that will work for you.

Maybe you feel uncomfortable going out alone, but try this: Go to the movies by yourself (you wouldn't talk to another person during the movie anyway) and enjoy the feeling of being alone in the dark, seeing exactly the movie you want to see.

These kinds of details really are the small stuff. As your brain detoxes from that "I need a partner to complete me" obsession, it's going to use those details to try to convince you that you can't stand being single. It will tell you these details are huge and cannot be overcome—except with a partner. But they really can. Millions of people live happily single every day. Some are hoping that one day they'll meet the perfect partner, some are taking a break from partnering, and some have consciously chosen to be single. (Katherine Hepburn once said, "Sometimes I wonder if men and women really suit each other. Perhaps they should live next door and just visit now and then.") All of them have figured out how to eat, play, and go out and have meaningful lives while being fabulously single. You can too. There are so many blogs and books about how to get comfortable going out, and even traveling on your own, that you'll find plenty of resources.

What we want to talk about here is silencing that voice in your head, the one that keeps making excuses for why being single won't work. You do it by redirecting your thoughts, reestablishing your connections, refocusing your purpose, and renewing your spirit.

EXERCISE 3. SILENCE THE VOICE OF YOUR ADDICTION

That inner voice, the one that keeps telling you that you can't survive as a single person, is the voice of your addiction. It will never run out of excuses. But in the end, that voice is a voice in *your* head, which means you can take control of it. One way is by being mindful. Notice when that voice starts coming up with excuses. Rather than getting caught up in what the voice is saying, just notice it. Say to yourself, "Oh, that's the voice of my addiction trying to convince me I can't do this. But I know I can."

Does that seem too simple? Well, it is simple, but it isn't. Noticing what your inner voice is saying—in a cool and detached way—is not so easy. That voice has been controlling your emotions all your life, and it's hard not to listen to it. But when you practice mindfulness (which really just means noticing your thoughts as a neutral observer), you become aware that what the voice is saying is only a story you're telling yourself. It doesn't have to be true. Change your beliefs about what being single means and you change the story.

Another way to silence the voice of your addiction is to make a list of all the excuses it's coming up with, and then write down the solutions. If you can't think of a solution right away, do some research.

Do you hate eating out alone? You can go out with friends sometimes, and sometimes get take-out. Do you have trouble doing simple home repairs? You can hire a handyman; your local hardware store or a home supply store can make recommendations, or you can try an online referral service such as TaskRabbit. Love to go out dancing? Go with some girlfriends, and see who you meet at the dance club. Can't take care of your car? Ask a neighbor or friend to recommend a good mechanic. Don't like hiking alone? Join a local chapter of the Sierra Club or another hiking group. Meetup.com lists all sorts of activity groups you can join, no matter what you're into.

For every problem, there's a solution. There *really is*. Don't let the voice of your addiction shut you down. Instead, tell it to shut up.

REDIRECT, REFOCUS, RENEW

An important aspect of living fabulously on your own is to get in touch with and align your mind, body, and spirit. You've been putting your partner—or your search for a partner—at the top of your priority list for too long. It's time to put yourself at the top of the list, reconnect with who you are and what you need and want. It's time to pamper yourself rather than pampering your partner.

Book a package of massages or facials or Reiki sessions or mani-pedis to pamper yourself physically. Start eating and sleeping well to nourish your body. Do not underestimate how important rest is for rejuvenating. We all need different amounts of sleep, so it's about finding what works for you.

Another way to pamper your body and reconnect mind and body is through acupuncture, which is an ancient Chinese practice that facilitates the flow of life energy (known as qi) through the body. I (Sherry) am a practitioner of Thought Field Therapy (TFT), which I often use with my clients to break negative thought patterns and behaviors. TFT uses a tapping sequence in the form of a healing code; this balances the body's energy system and helps dissipate negative emotions.

Both TFT and acupuncture help remove blocks in our bodies, changing the way we see things. Often we get stuck in negative thought loops, and by moving energy to unblock certain points, we can correct imbalances. These practices have been shown to be very effective in treating all sorts of addictions.

Pamper yourself spiritually, too. Adding spirituality to your life does not necessarily mean organized religion—although if that speaks to you, by all means get involved with a church, synagogue, mosque, temple, or sangha. But remember that spirituality is more about your connection to something greater than yourself. It is about connecting with a force that speaks to you, whether it's a higher power, God, Allah, Buddha, Jesus, the universe, the force, or infinite intelligence. Spirituality is discovering why you are here and what brings meaning to your life.

Some ways to do that is through soulful activities, such as meditation, prayer, energy medicine, getting into nature, and being sexual. All these things can restore your life force and spiritual energy. These activities move you away from relationship addiction, fantasy, and obsession and closer to your true spirit—the one that can nurture you on its own.

Meditation decreases stress and helps you become mindful of your thoughts. It assists in taming your monkey mind, where your thoughts are out to get you. A meditation practice can bring peace to all those thoughts of, "When will I meet someone? What if I am alone forever? I can't do this alone," and all the other things the voice of addiction keeps repeating in your head. (You can learn more about meditation in the Appendix.) If a regular meditation practice isn't your thing, set the timer on your phone to beep every ninety minutes. When it does, stop whatever you're doing and take three slow, deep breaths in through your nose and out through your mouth. Just center yourself.

Getting out into the natural world is another way of reconnecting with your spiritual side. Being in nature is food for our souls. We spend way too much time indoors engaging with technology and way too little time breathing in the beauty of our natural environments. Go to a park and take a brisk walk, get out of the city and hike, collect seashells, swim in a natural body of water, or simply bird watch.

Creativity is an aspect of renewal. Whether it's taking up a musical instrument, listening to music, singing, writing, knitting, painting, taking an acting class, dancing, journaling, or blogging, all these things are great ways to express yourself and tap into your streams of consciousness. When you give up your addiction, you need to replace it with something that will nurture you and bring you joy. If not, you are more likely to go back to a past unhealthy relationship or to look for a new love object to obsess over. Have a creative pursuit, rather than a partner pursuit. It's a way of expressing self-care and of exploring your own truth.

EXERCISE 4. GET MOVING

Movement of all kinds does wonders for the mind, body, and spirit by creating feelings of euphoria. Doctors report that exercise greatly improves symptoms of depression and anxiety. In other words, movement is a natural high.

It can be as simple as a walk around the block or a few minutes of stretching in front of the television. We humans tend to be very black and white in our thinking and believe exercise has to be long and difficult or must be done at the gym. The truth is, any sort of movement improves health and well-being.

There are so many wonderful ways to include walking in your life, such as forming a walking group, walking with your friends, parking your car a long distance from where you are headed, or taking the stairs instead of the elevator. If you're watching your child's softball or soccer game, you can walk around the field instead of sitting on the sidelines.

By exercising, you are less likely to obsess about your love object or daydream about your next great love. When you are exercising or pursuing an activity you enjoy, you are in the flow. The flow is where you are in the present—not thinking about the past or future tripping about what might be. You are right here, right now, not obsessing about past partners or future partners.

We are certainly not suggesting you become addicted to exercise (and if you find it's getting in the way of other areas of your life, you may need to take a look at that). What we are suggesting is adding balance to your life, and one way to do that is through exercise.

When I (Sherry) went through my fourth divorce, I took up outrigger canoeing. It was the best thing I could have done for myself. It got me out of the house. I paddled with other people, which provided connection for me. It was in the water, which brought me closer to nature, and it was fun. I can't tell you how much canoeing shifted my mindset from obsessiveness to serenity. Being one with the ebb and flow of the water, to me, is a form of meditation.

It is important to find a type of exercise that you enjoy, or else you're unlikely to stick with it. Try an introductory class in spinning, Zumba, tai chi, yoga, Pilates, strength training, aerobics, or whatever seems fun to you. All of these exercises are great for your body, your health, and your well-being and are healthy distractions from the cycle of relationship addiction.

BREAK UP WITH YOUR DATING APP

If you're learning to live fabulously on your own, that's where your energy needs to go. We know people say they're on an app just to see what's out there, but if you're a relationship addict, dating apps reinforce all the ideas you need to get away from.

As you are learning in this chapter, you don't always need to be dating. These apps stay in business by reinforcing social stereotypes that people need to be paired up to be happy and that being in a relationship *must* be everyone's ultimate goal. In real life, you can be happy alone or miserable in a relationship. Or it could be the other way around. Happiness does not depend on pairing up.

In their advertisements, dating apps also promote the idea of "happily ever after." That's a fantasy. And if there's one thing relationship addicts need to stop fantasizing about, it's that the perfect partner will sweep them up into the perfect romance, so they can live happily ever after. Real-life couples have happy times and tough times, times when they want to be together every moment and times when a little goes a long way. They know they will never get everything they need in life from just one relationship.

Having unrealistic expectations about a partner is a recipe for disappointment and disaster. No one can save you or turn around your life by being perfect for you. You're responsible for your own life, and only *you* can make it great or make it miserable—or somewhere on that wide spectrum in between where most of us live.

That hot but sensitive guy or cute but no-nonsense woman in the dating app commercial does not hold the key to your happiness. You do. But dating apps keep tempting you to believe otherwise.

Let's consider an example using a more well-known addiction— gambling. If you fantasize that being rich is the only way to be happy, and that the best way to get rich is to play casino slot machines, you're going to spend all your free time and all your money playing slot machines— becoming poor and unfulfilled and never truly being happy. That's time you could have spent actually working to earn some money and energy you could have invested in figuring out what you're good at and passionate about to make a successful career for yourself.

Likewise, if you keep playing the dating app slot machine, you're going to invest all your time and energy chasing a fantasy relationship, rather than figuring out what's really going to make you happy and then going about getting it.

We're not saying don't date; we're saying don't work on dating. Work on building a life for yourself that's fine whether you are dating or not.

EXERCISE 5. CELEBRATE

Celebrating life and your authentic self can be anything from gathering for a special meal to taking a mini vacation to attending a spiritual retreat. Celebrations bring people together and take you away from your usual routines. Focusing on your celebration pulls you away from your addiction triggers. It puts you in a place where you can relax, rejuvenate, and regroup. Celebrations can be a day trip, a spa day, a picnic, a day at the beach, or a hike in nature. The point is to remove yourself from your typical environment, so you can gain a new perspective about where you have been, where you are now, and where you are going—both in and out of relationships.

SEX AND THE SINGLE PERSON

Another aspect of connecting with mind, body, and spirit is sexuality. We are not talking about sex addiction here, which can be a part of relationship addiction, but rather intimacy and connection. Connecting physically through touch, such as hugging, kissing and sex, decreases our stress hormones, improves our mood, and allows us to feel more joy, peace, and hope. It is another way of releasing endorphins, which reduce anxiety.

Living fabulously on your own may mean a period of abstinence. It may mean experimenting with unencumbered sexual partners outside of a committed relationship, or even same-sex partners. Exploring your sexuality as a single person can be fluid.

Of course, these encounters need to be safe—using protection, meeting in safe places, and knowing who you are meeting or choosing to sleep with. You also need to be completely honest with your partners, so no one has emotional expectations that cannot be met. You don't want to hurt someone else in the process of exploring your own sexuality. The important thing here is to explore all sides of your sexual self without shame or judgment.

We have both experimented in these areas at different times of our lives, which allowed us to explore hidden aspects of ourselves that were longing to be discovered. When I (Sherry) had encounters that were primarily physical later in life, they fulfilled longings and desires kept hidden away out of fear of what others might think of me or label me. In reality, they were just different reflections of how I saw myself. I carried shame around these parts of me, and I thought it was easier to just deny and ignore these long-lost desires than to act on them. When I went through my fourth divorce, I had the courage to step into this aspect of myself, and I will forever be grateful I did.

I met the most interesting women and men, who I would never have met otherwise. I came to understand sexuality is fluid and ever-expanding. I realized that sexuality is part of a continuum, and that our sexual selves can move along this continuum at different times in our lives. The important thing is not to judge that continuum or deny where you are on it.

In addition, you need not label yourself. We are ever-changing beings—growing, creating, and becoming more of who we are when we don't fear stepping outside of the default zone we have created for ourselves. So go ahead, take that step, go to the edge of your discomfort, and you will be greatly surprised about what will be revealed.

RECONNECT

When we talk about mind, body, and spirit, what we are really talking about is connection. The need to connect is in our DNA; humans are social animals. One of the reasons we become addicted to relationships is the need to connect. Although the addiction itself stems from a natural desire to connect, the connection is usually unhealthy. We need to find healthier connections—ones that are based on love, respect, and compassion, not desperation.

That connection might be family, friends, colleagues, community, worship, recreational groups, or even political affiliations. Having connections decreases your sense of isolation; it takes you out of your own self-absorption or neediness, and that can strengthen your self-esteem. At the same time, by having a community, you are less likely to rely on one person to meet all your needs. You might end up with a friend you hike with, a friend you shop with, a friend you eat with, and a friend you cry with.

If you were neglected by your parents or early caregivers, connecting with others can be more difficult because you may find it difficult to trust. When it's hard to trust anyone, your instinct is to turn to just one person, your love object, to meet all your needs. But as you already know, one person can never meet all your needs. These unhealthy bonds, based on mistrust and extreme need, create a sense of false connection. The more comfortable you become in your skin, the more likely it is that you will be able to relate to others in healthier ways.

Share your vulnerabilities with others and let them know you are lonely or need some extra tender loving care, rather than clinging to one unhealthy love object. There are so many ways to connect today with others, such as Meetup groups, women's groups, sports fun leagues, book clubs, or whatever group resonates with your interests and hobbies.

Reconnect with old friends through texting, Facebook, Twitter, and other social media outlets. While it's great to use social media to keep in touch, don't let it become a substitute for real-world connections. We need to be with people, to hug them and sit across from them at the table and laugh with them. We need friends to go to dinner with and go bike riding and shopping together.

Twelve-step meetings, such as Sex and Love Addicts Anonymous and Codependents Anonymous, are great ways to connect by healing those broken places inside of us and by making supportive and accepting connections.

I will never forget when I (Sherry) joined Al-Anon and met others who had an alcoholic in their life. It didn't matter if it was their child, parent, or a significant other; what mattered was, I could relate to their stories. It helped me feel less alone and allowed me to take the focus off my alcoholic husband and put it on my own wants and needs.

There is a narcissistic quality that creeps in when you are in the midst of an addiction to someone else. By going to meetings, getting a sponsor, and sponsoring others, you are part of a process of giving and receiving.

You give to others who are on a similar journey and, in turn, receive love and acceptance from others in the program.

NO EXPLANATION NEEDED

As we discussed in chapter 1, there's a lot of social pressure to be in a relationship. Everyone around us seems to think it's their business, and they ask questions, offer advice, and even try to set us up on dates. When you're a relationship addict working on feeling good about living on your own, that kind of pressure is the last thing you need.

For all the talk about tolerance and inclusion, we live in a society where it's tough to be a nonconformist on the basics. We're expected to be in a relationship, we're expected to eventually get married, we're expected to have children, and we're expected to explain ourselves when we don't.

I (Beth) don't have any children. The reasons for this are very personal and, since I've been married twice, kind of complex. As personal as this decision has been for me in both my marriages, a lot of people think it's their business. I went through two and half decades of, "When are you having kids?" When I hit my fifties and the answer was obviously "never," I assumed the question would finally fade away. But it hasn't. It's just morphed into, "Why didn't you ever have kids?"

Our society says if you don't conform to a typical life path, there's something wrong with you. Your parents say so, your friends say so, and the cultural institutions around you say so. Relationship addicts have internalized those rules so deeply that they cannot feel comfortable unless they follow them.

This is especially true for women. Just think about the words we use in Western culture: Single men who have many casual relationships are playboys, lady-killers, or tomcats. Women who do the same are sluts, whores, or cougars. Unmarried men are bachelors, even into middle age, while unmarried middle-aged women are spinsters—a word that's said in a sad, sympathetic whisper. We imagine them friendless and alone in their old age.

There's a lot of social judgment in those words. And social judgment is hard to go against, especially when you look outside yourself for your sense of worth, as relationship addicts do. "I don't give a damn what anyone thinks" is easier said than done.

"When are you going to find someone?" That question is so loaded, so personal, so hurtful, that it can make you feel unworthy and ashamed. It always takes you by surprise, and it's often easier to apologize for not following social conventions than it is to stand up for yourself.

You need to stop offering explanations, because doing so implies that you're somehow in the wrong. There's absolutely nothing wrong with being single. Embrace it with joy—no explanation needed.

What really helps with questions like that is to have a handful of answers ready. Write them down, and practice saying them so they come out easily and naturally—a quick rejoinder that you don't even have to think about. You'll be amazed at how much better you feel when you can answer that question with an answer that validates you and your choices.

Here are a few ideas. Some are a little snarky, some are not, because different people and different situations call for different kinds of responses. So, when are you going to find someone?

» Why would you ask that?

» I don't need to.

» I have a lot of other things going on that keep me busy.

» Why don't you tell me something private about yourself first?

» It's not on the top of my to-do list.

» I am waiting to meet the right person.

» Because I deserve the best, and that takes time.

EXERCISE 6. GIVE SOMETHING BACK

There is nothing more powerful than giving. It's one of the foundations of every 12-step program. By helping others, you are getting out of your own way and being of service to others who are going through the same process. Giving can include supporting a charity, either by donating funds or by participating in various events. Other types of giving include volunteer work, or cleaning out your closet, your garage, your whole home and donating all the usable items to a charity resale shop. The sense of cleansing you get when you do this is positively purifying.

Giving back makes you feel more confident about your own worth—you have something worth giving and something worth receiving. When you are feeling more confident, you attract others of like mind back into your life. You have a much better chance of widening your social circle when you are feeling positive about yourself.

CHAPTER 9

DATING WITHOUT DESPERATION

When it comes to matters of the heart, it's no easy thing to get out into the world and make yourself vulnerable. If you have shaky self-esteem, all the issues that arose from your early trauma can surface again when you start dating, so treat the process mindfully, listen to your intuition, and be discerning. Most importantly, be honest with yourself and with the people you go out with. If your only goal is a hookup to avoid loneliness or a distraction to avoid boredom, say so. It's okay, as long as you tell the truth right from the start.

Be prepared spiritually and emotionally to begin the process of dating. If you are still healing from relationship addiction or haven't gotten over a past relationship, now is not the time to start dating. You will just be bringing your baggage to your dating experiences, which will certainly not lead you to the partner of your dreams. Remember, dating isn't a Band-Aid for old wounds or a way to get your parents off your back; it's a process that should be treated consciously and respectfully.

EXERCISE 1. AN EMOTIONAL INVENTORY

Partners in a healthy relationship know who they are, feel good about themselves, and are ready to be in a relationship. Are you emotionally ready to start a healthy relationship? Circle the statements that apply to you.

1. I am worthy despite my faults.

2. I am responsible.

3. I am authentic.

4. I live by my values.

5. I am trustworthy.

6. I am open with my feelings.

7. I am not clingy.

8. I am not afraid of being alone.

9. I can be alone without always feeling lonely.

10. I participate in life.

11. I don't give up my interests for another person.

12. I am good to myself.

13. I believe in give and take in relationships.

14. I am assertive.

15. I have boundaries.

16. I am working on myself.

17. I have healthy associations.

18. I am whole.

19. Rejection does not make me spin out of control.

20. I don't take things personally.

21. I've worked through my childhood issues.

22. I can remove myself from unhealthy relationships.

23. I'm comfortable in a healthy relationship.

24. When a relationship is over, I know I can move on.

25. I have balance in my life.

26. I've learned how to let go.

If you have circled most of these statements, you are ready for a healthy relationship. If you have circled just a few of these statements, then you are dating for all the wrong reasons and are setting yourself up for an unhealthy relationship. You still have work to do, an inner child to nurture, and wounds to heal.

THE ONE THING YOU ABSOLUTELY NEED TO FIND A GREAT PARTNER

We'll admit, that sounds kind of like an ad for perfume or positivity or plastic surgery. But you don't need to go shopping for the one thing you absolutely need to find a great partner. Because—surprise!—what you really need is to know in your heart that you're just fine on your own.

That means you're secure in yourself, you've built a life you enjoy, and nobody else is going to complete you. A partner would be wonderful, but only the *right* partner. Until/unless you find them, you can date for fun and friendship, hang out with your friends and family, and complete yourself.

How strongly do we feel about this? As long as you feel you can't live *without* a partner, you shouldn't live *with* a partner. We say that because it's really impossible to have a healthy relationship when you're desperate to get paired up. Authentic partnerships are based on respect and trust and shared values—not desperation.

Desperation makes you unattractive to well-grounded, self-assured people (the people you should be looking for), and an easy mark for those who want to take advantage of you. It keeps you in relationships you know will never really work out, long after they have turned sour. And that's a recipe for a lifetime of settling for less than you want and deserve.

Desperation sets in when you believe you need a partner to be happy. But you are setting yourself up for relationship failure and disappointment when you believe someone else is responsible for your well-being. Thinking that way stops you from setting healthy boundaries and asking for what you need and want. It prevents you from being your authentic self in a relationship.

The right partner would add to your life—we don't deny that. But a partner can't sustain your life. Only *you* can do that. You're already whole, with or without a partner. That means you can happily bide your time and wait until the right one comes along. So . . . the first step in dating and creating an authentic partnership with someone who will value you for who you are and treat you the way you deserve is to kick your addiction and learn to live fabulously on your own. If you're not there yet, take some more time to work through chapter 8.

WHAT DO YOU WANT? WHAT DO YOU NEED?

If you're not looking to be in a relationship just to heal old wounds or to fill a void in your life, what are you looking for? And if you're not going to try to change your partner to make them "perfect," who do they need to be? These are big questions, and they require thoughtful answers.

It's time to make a vision statement. The clearer you are, the better chance you have of meeting that person. Make sure your inventory is not superficial, though—just looks, status, and wealth. Things like what car a person drives, how tall they are, what type of career they have, or how much money they make may appear attractive, but they tell you nothing about a person's character. Real attraction is what grows when you get to know a person's substance and values.

If your desire is someone with a large bank account and sculpted abs, go ahead and write that down in your vision statement. However, we're not quite sure those things will bring you everlasting love. If you are just picking up on the "shiny object" attributes of a partner, that's all you'll get. Someone who is attracted to shiny objects leaves as soon as there's someone else available who's younger, richer, smarter, more attractive. Is that who you want to be? Is that who you want to date?

That's why truly knowing who someone is from the inside out is so important. You want to be able to find someone with whom you can build a relationship in which you both articulate your feelings directly and honestly. You want to find someone who respects the independence you have worked so hard to build but also cares for you and doesn't exploit the vulnerable parts of who you are.

Make a list of the character traits and values you are looking for in a person. Often, they will be very similar to your own. You've already spent a lot of time taking an inventory of yourself and rethinking your values. Who are you now that you are breaking free of your relationship addiction? You want to date someone who is the kind of person you are becoming.

Once you've considered the big issues, it's time to think about the details. What do you like to do for fun? What type of music do you enjoy? What kinds of foods do you like to eat? Do you like to cook? What sports do you enjoy? What type of vacations are fun for you? Are you an ocean person or a mountain person? What kinds of movie do you love? What kinds do you hate? Are you looking for someone fit who likes physical activities or a couch potato? Shared interests can bring couples together, but they're not vital. If you don't share interests with someone you like, ask yourself if you are willing to do activities you enjoy on your own or with other friends.

Think, too, about social styles. Do they like pets, are they spiritual, are they close with their family? When you go out on a date, do you want them to pay or should you each pick up your own check? What sort of political affiliations do they have, do they smoke, are they an introvert or extrovert? My (Sherry's) ex-husband was an introvert, and when we did go out with other people, he was awkward and withdrawn. We ended up staying home a lot because that's what made him comfortable, and I lost many valuable friendships.

This may be the first time in your life that your criteria for who you are looking for includes something other than "loves and nurtures me obsessively." Enjoy the experience of making a list of what you like and don't like and looking for someone who measures up.

When you make your list of attributes, know where your line in the sand is about what is totally unacceptable in a potential partner. Don't cross it, no matter how tempting a date seems. (See chapter 10 for more about setting boundaries.)

If you're a single parent, you definitely want to know about their child-rearing ideas. When I (Sherry) was a single mom, I mostly dated men who didn't have children and had never given them much thought. Unfortunately, they didn't have a clue about parenting and didn't understand the sacrifices you make when you become a parent. This caused many issues for my daughter and me. Honestly, if I could do it all over again, I would be more open to dating other single parents.

BECOME THE PERSON YOU WANT TO ATTRACT

As we said in chapter 7, the way you think and act invites who and what you will bring into your life. This is the time to review what messages you received while growing up about relationships. What did your parents tell you about love? Did they follow their desires? Did they do what they should do, or what their hearts told them? Were they stifled or did they grow in their relationship? Are you attracting partners who mirror your parents' relationship?

The answers to these questions should help you understand what you bring forth into your life. Do you block love by the messages you tell yourself? Do you say out loud that you want to find love but internally tell yourself it will never happen for you? What you truly believe is what the universe will give you. Mixed messages will never get you what you want.

The universe listens for congruency. If what you believe and how you act in the world do not match, the lack of congruency sabotages your results. For example, if in your core you truly do not believe you deserve a healthy relationship but continue to go on dates hoping to meet "the one," you are putting out conflicting energy. On the other hand, if you believe healthy love is on its way and you project that out in the world, you have a much better chance of making it so.

Start living as if you already have love in your life. When you expect things to be different, you will start attracting different energy—and different people. There is always space and time to reinvent yourself and what it is you desire.

After my fourth divorce, I (Sherry) was done dating and started participating in positive activities for myself. I stopped trying so hard to find a man, and instead, just tried to live a happy life. Suddenly, the right people and circumstances started showing up in my life. When you let go of your relationship addiction, you become more interested in non-codependent and nourishing relationships. I have made lifelong meaningful and fulfilling friendships. Align yourself with people, places, and things that resonate with love, hopefulness, and joy. You never know who you will meet while hanging around good and joyful people.

There is nothing wrong with envisioning what your life might feel like when you find that healthy partner. It is the desperate neediness that you must have someone that creates negative energy. Turn desperation into knowing and certainty that the right partner is just around the corner. Express gratitude that the right love for you is on its way. Your higher power will make it so. Become the person you wish to attract.

DATING APPS

In our grandparents' day, couples were typically introduced by family and friends. In today's dating world, though, there are seemingly endless options for meeting people: single vacations, meet-ups, networking events, charity events, continuing education, speed dating, and the most popular today, dating apps. The list of apps keeps growing and changing, and it can be pretty intimidating. How do you know where to begin?

Just pick one, and get on it. Try one that gives you a free trial, if you can. Users often rate dating apps based on which seem to be more serious and which seem to be places where people are just looking for sex. Pick a more serious one, set aside an hour, and set up a profile.

Don't make it feel like a job, because if you do, that's the type of energy you will be putting into your profile and out into the universe. Try to have a little fun with it—that's a much better kind of energy to manifest. But most important, be honest. You've left behind those days of trying to twist yourself into whoever you think someone else wants. Be authentic in your profile, and someone who is attracted to who you truly are will find you.

It's important to also post photos that truly reflect who you are today. Many men have told me that the photos of the dates they were meeting were often inaccurate. And believe me, I (Sherry) went on many dates where the guy was at least twenty years older than his photos reflected. It was disappointing and very dishonest. This is not a great way to start any relationship.

By the way, try to keep those photos with your pets to a minimum. Listen, Sherry loves her two dogs and Beth loves her two cats, but it's a turn-off to post photos with them. Try to post current photos in which you are relaxed and enjoying yourself, and that reflect positive energy.

Start out just dating in your local area. You've spent a lot of time building up a support network of people you trust, and you'll need them in your life as you begin dating. Also, sometimes when you begin a long-distance relationship, you build up a fantasy about who that person is because you don't see them that often. And fantasizing about partners is the last thing you need.

From time to time put some new information on your profile, so you will rise a bit higher in searches. But don't spend a lot of time on this, and do it thoughtfully. Check your app once a day to see if there's anyone you'd like to meet or anyone who would like to meet you. If you find yourself checking it more often, schedule in some app-checking time once a day, and stick to your schedule. Remember, dating is *one part* of your very rich and full life—it's not the goal of your life.

FIRST DATES

Before you meet someone in person, try to talk on the phone first. Keep the conversation short and sweet; your goal here is to figure out whether or not you want to actually meet them. This is not the time to share your greatest secrets. If you have any intuition that this is not a good fit for you, move on. So often we try to convince ourselves to meet someone we know is not right. That's called denial: We want to pair up so desperately that we ignore all the red flags. But this time, you're dating without desperation. If it doesn't feel right, don't make a date.

If you do decide to make a date, keep it simple. Meet for a cup of coffee or an ice cream. Make sure you choose a public place with lots of people around. Let a friend or family member know where you are going, for safety reasons. Don't choose a bar, because drinking and driving is a no-no. Plus, sometimes drinking alcohol can make anyone look good. Going to someone's house or inviting them to yours on a first date is also a big no-no, especially for safety reasons but also to avoid the awkwardness of having sex too quickly.

Dress as yourself. If you are a free spirit and don't wear makeup (or never wear a jacket and tie), don't wear it on the first date just to impress. Present yourself as authentically as possible, so you can start to get a good read on whether you are truly compatible.

Notice the energy flowing between you. Is your date is making assumptions about you or do they appear to have unreasonably high expectations? This type of person will never be satisfied. Another red flag is whether your date is looking at you or checking out other people.

Ask questions rather than just talk about yourself, and take notice of whether your date is doing the same thing. When someone just goes on and on about themselves, they might be self-centered or even a narcissist. Make your questions count, and don't be afraid to ask things that will give you insight into who this person is.

Do they appear to be financially secure? Again, that doesn't mean rich; it just means they can take care of themselves. Don't pass up a great person based on what kind of car they drive, what their career is, or how expensive their clothes are. Remember, dating isn't about creating fantasies; rather, it's about being open to looking beyond someone's image or even their physical attractiveness.

EXERCISE 2. FIRST DATE CHARACTER CHECK

One of the most important things you want to look for during that first date is whether or not the person sitting in front of you is a person of character. Some questions you might ask yourself:

» Does this person only talk about themselves or are they also interested in me?

» Is this person courteous?

» Is this person polite?

» Is this person kind?

» Is this person selfish?

» Does this person seem loyal or are they badmouthing the people they know?

» Does this person seem honest?

» Does this person seem open but also independent?

» Does this person have their own set of interests?

TAKE IT SLOW ... SLOWER ... SLOWEST

We've talked a lot about how love at first sight is really a fantasy fed by a romance addiction. Slow and steady is the way you fall in love with someone. Those giddy feelings when you first meet someone you are attracted to are fleeting; when you start to think they mean you're already in a real relationship, it never works out.

If you find you're attracted to someone on a first date and the feeling seems to be mutual, stick to "like at first sight." This is someone worth getting to know. No butterflies or fantasies about moving in together; just, "What a nice person. I'd like to see them again."

If you feel yourself slipping back into that fantasy world, pull out some of the exercises you have been doing in the earlier chapters and reread what you wrote. You've come a long way since you started this book. Be mindful of what you've learned, so you don't relapse into your addiction.

It's worth pointing out that there's a difference between infatuation and true love. This is probably something you know in your head, but not always in your heart. Infatuation is an illusion of who you think someone is, rather than who they really are. It's the state of unreality where everything about a date feels perfect. Saying you're in love with someone you've only been out with once or twice is kind of like saying you love a celebrity: You love the image they project and the fantasy that sparks within you, rather than the actual person. In other words, it's impossible to fall in love on a first or second date. You can't get to know a person that quickly.

WRESTLING WITH REJECTION

Dating in the digital age is a slippery slope for the relationship addict, especially if you have not done the work to heal yourself. Dating on an app is often a numbers game, with so many opportunities to meet someone new with just a swipe. The nature of the digital dating process leaves many baffled and confused when someone doesn't reciprocate their attraction or ghosts them (ignores all their attempts to get in touch). Sherry has worked with many clients who take it very personally if someone shows no interest or doesn't call back—even when they themselves agree they didn't hit it off.

Finding someone in the dating pool is a subtle dance between letting go of the outcome and being open to possibilities. Remember, one of the problems relationship addicts have is believing an illusion about who someone is, rather than who they really are. Freeing yourself from addiction means freeing yourself from those illusions. Dating needs to be a conscious process of getting to know someone with discernment, compassion, openness, and self-love, rather than desperation. Awareness is the nexus of power.

This is where surrendering to your higher power can help. It's human nature to feel uncomfortable with the unknown, but it is in the unknown that infinite possibilities exist. Even in the discomfort of not knowing if this is someone you want to go on date number two with, you need to stay conscious and crawl "in like" rather than fall in love.

If you feel discomfort overtaking your common sense, slow it down and notice in your body where you are feeling this craving. Ask yourself:

» Am I looking for someone to fill me up?

» Do I not feel whole as I am?

» Am I looking to get what I never received as a child?

» Am I in falling into fantasy and illusion?

» Am I confusing infatuation and sexual attraction with real love?

» Am I ignoring the red flags?

If the answer to any of these questions is "yes," bring yourself back to the present moment, be mindful, and remind yourself that all is well *right now*. That doesn't mean you can't be cautiously optimistic; it just means you are allowing excitement to coexist with realism. Remember, some of the best things in life take time.

CHAPTER 10

CREATING AUTHENTIC PARTNERSHIPS AND EVERLASTING LOVE

We've talked a lot in the previous chapters about how relationship addicts end up falling in love with a fantasy about what partnerships are or are supposed to be. There's nothing authentic about loving a fantasy, and there's nothing authentic about twisting yourself into someone you think your partner wants you to be. In authentic partnerships, you are always your authentic self.

It's also a fantasy to think that any relationship will enable you to relive your childhood in a better way or find someone who can re-parent you. Your childhood is past. No one gets a do-over. What you do get is a chance at a healthy relationship that can lead to real, everlasting love.

WHAT DO HEALTHY RELATIONSHIPS LOOK LIKE?

Healthy relationships are not rooted in fantasy. Both partners have realistic expectations about how much happiness should come from the relationship. They know that in all relationships, there are days when things will feel incredibly exciting and days when the relationship will feel ordinary; it's not all or nothing, intoxicating romance or unbearable pain.

Compatibility and ease in a relationship come from being alike or having a high tolerance of differences. Healthy couples are sexually compatible, meaning they have similar preferences and ideas about what makes for good sex. They also have similar values about things like money, religion, monogamy, and parenting—although they certainly do not have to be identical. When it comes to family, the traditions and rituals of each partner's family must be renegotiated—so both partners need to be flexible enough to do that—and the couple will create some of their own rituals and traditions.

In all relationships, couples have their ups and downs. They disagree, they sometimes even argue, but there is a basic willingness to negotiate and compromise, to face problems together without over-reacting, and to make sacrifices now and then. When they fight, healthy couples fight fair, expressing their opinions without attacking the other person. They do not dish out or tolerate abuse. They listen as well as talk, and they are role models for each other, rather than nags.

Each partner is able to ask for what they want. They say what they mean, directly but with sensitivity. It is this kind of honesty that engenders trust.

Healthy couples spend quality time together and quality time apart. They share some interests, but they do not share every moment. They have fun together and fun with other friends. They also have personal boundaries that their partner respects. There is patience and tolerance, a give and take.

THE LINE IN THE SAND—SETTING BOUNDARIES

Boundaries tell us where we stop and another person begins. They are the lines that separate us from others. They give us the opportunity to embrace a secure sense of self as someone separate from others. If we grow up in a healthy family system, we have the chance to build a healthy sense of self. If we grow up in a family where we were abused, neglected, shamed, or abandoned, we didn't learn appropriate boundaries.

Relationship junkies generally grew up in families where boundaries were hazy at best. One example is a family with one or more substance abusers; these are families where parents are generally emotionally and physically unavailable. Often, these parents will expect their children to handle responsibilities way beyond their age. These children learn that there are no boundaries to what may be expected of them.

Setting good boundaries prevents extremes in relationships, such as being too close or too distant, giving too much or too little, idealizing or devaluing others. None of these extremes are healthy. Sherry often tells clients that a boundary is the gate around my front yard that keeps positive stuff in and negative stuff out.

The inability to set boundaries is a misguided attempt to be loved. In his book, *Healing the Shame That Binds You*, John Bradshaw wrote, "Only when we have good boundaries can we expand our boundaries with someone else. Only when we have strong boundaries can we love." When a sense of self is not respected, boundaries become nonexistent, and relationship junkies become over-givers as adults. When boundaries are blurred, the feelings and behaviors of others become the addict's own. There is no dividing line between where the addict ends and others begin.

Relationship junkies are easily trampled on out of a need to please. They describe their relationships as if the other person is living inside their skin. There is a desperate need to merge with their partner.

Some examples of boundary violations include:

» Having deep conversations with others you hardly know
» Falling in love and/or getting involved without really knowing someone
» Trusting too easily
» Staying in relationships long after they have turned sour

» Intruding on others' boundaries (checking a partner's personal belongings, cell phone, texts, e-mails)

» Stalking

» Having promiscuous sex just to please others

» Touching another person without their permission or letting them touch you

» Letting others tell you how to live your life

» Flirting with others just to make a connection

» Expecting another person to know your needs without expressing them

The way to develop healthy boundaries is to learn how to set limits with others. Sometimes it means leaving a situation or expressing what you need, rather than submitting to another's whims. Nurturing the inner child within is a great way to regain the loss of self and create boundaries (see chapter 6).

The next step is learning to distinguish the lines between you and those you love. Once you do this, you will see that you are not responsible for what other people do. So often, relationship junkies believe they are responsible for someone else's inappropriate behavior, such as abuse, addictions, cheating, and/or unlawful activity. We are responsible only for ourselves. Everyone must own their actions.

You know you are gaining a stronger sense of self and developing boundaries when you realize "No" is a complete sentence; you don't have to explain or defend yourself. You stop feeling guilty, stop believing everything that's not perfect in your relationships is your fault. You realize you are not responsible for the behavior of others, and become just as comfortable giving as you are receiving. You learn to differentiate your needs from others' needs and begin to feel a sense of safety being you. You honor your own feelings; ask for what you need; are not afraid to have a different opinion; know what is someone else's business and what is yours;

learn to nurture yourself; do what you want to do without depending on another's suggestions; stop blaming yourself for everything that isn't right in your relationship; and know how to set limits. When you set boundaries, you create space for the right person to show up in your life.

EXERCISE 1. SETTING BOUNDARIES IN ONE RELATIONSHIP

Think about a relationship where you need to set clear boundaries, then go through this whole exercise thinking about that one person. Share your decisions with them.

_____

(Name of person you are setting the boundary with)

_____

(Your reason for setting the boundary)

_____

(What the boundary is)

The purpose of setting boundaries is to take care of your needs and to protect yourself from inappropriate behavior, so you don't feel victimized by someone else's actions. Only set limits that you are willing to follow through with. Some boundaries may be more rigid than others.

Express your boundaries using a statement such as:

If you_____(behavior), I will take care of myself by _____(action).

If you_____(behavior), I will _____ (a way to confront that behavior and share my feelings).

If you continue that behavior, I will take care of myself by _____ (action).

For example:

For my self-esteem, I am no longer willing to enable you by accepting your infidelity/accepting your substance abuse/blaming myself for your behavior.

If you verbally or physically abuse me, I will take care of myself by leaving the situation.

If you blame me for your feelings, I will confront your blaming.

If you continue that behavior, I will take care of myself by ending the conversation.

EXERCISE 2. SETTING BROADER BOUNDARIES

Make a list of boundaries you can set with others and with yourself.

Boundary_____

With others_____

With myself _____

For example:

Boundary: Saying no.

With others: Don't go along with activities I don't want to engage in.

With myself: Don't fall in love blindly or trust so quickly.

TAKE IT SLOW

Love at first sight, or at least after the first date, is such a romantic idea. And it really does happen for some couples—or at least, later on they claim that it did. While they can look back a year later and say, "I knew right away," did they really? *Right away?* It sounds so sweet to say it, but you never hear people actually say it after their first date; it's something they say in hindsight. In reality, it takes time to get to know someone—to know if they are the right person for you.

That's especially true for recovering relationship junkies. They have a tendency to jump right over reality and straight to fantasy; right over what's happening now and straight to an imagined future. Recovering addicts need to take things slow and be mindful to stay in the now. Don't try to drive a relationship further and faster than it should be. Start with a healthy friendship and see where it goes all on its own.

If you've been trapped in the cycle of relationship addiction, you may not know how healthy relationships unfold naturally. A good start, as we said before, is having a healthy relationship with yourself. Know what you want, what you don't want, and what your boundaries are. If it helps to make things clear, write down a list of the qualities that are mandatory in a partner and the qualities that are optional. Be realistic, but don't settle for less than what you truly want and need.

As you start dating, do it with the idea of establishing friendships. Relax and have fun together. Measure your compatibility. Be yourself— your authentic self. You want someone to know who you *really* are and if you really are right for each other.

See if you can count on this person, but don't do it by setting tests and traps. Just let the friendship unfold naturally and you will see whether they are trustworthy and dependable. If you find that romantic feelings begin to grow within your friendship, so much the better. If not, it's great that you've found a new friend.

Hold off on sex because it can easily blind you, and keep a lid on those budding romantic feelings; don't give them a lot of power by fantasizing too much. Be willing to walk away if you usually cling to unhealthy people, and be willing to hang in there if you usually run.

As your romance blossoms, set ground rules for the relationship. Do this in a way that considers both persons' needs and boundaries and creates space for you to be together and be apart. Proceed at a pace that is comfortable for both of you, and don't worry if your partner's pace is different from yours. Give them the space to grow into the relationship. Maintain what you have and move forward when you both are ready. Discuss fidelity, the future, how much time you have for each other—

anything that is important to you. Honor the values you have in common; grow as a couple, as well as individuals.

EXERCISE 3. AM I IN A HEALTHY RELATIONSHIP?

When you do get into a romantic relationship, you may find it hard to trust your intuition. Have you finally figured who the good ones are? Was this one worth waiting for? This list of qualities should help.

Circle the statements that describe your current relationship. *I have chosen a partner who:*

1. Is honest
2. Is not afraid of commitment
3. Is cooperative
4. Is self-aware
5. Knows their own worth
6. Is a good communicator
7. Understands and nurtures their own inner child
8. Has similar values to mine
9. Is emotionally intelligent
10. Is not controlling
11. Has their own boundaries and respects mine
12. Has time for me
13. Is easy to be with
14. Is able to negotiate our differences
15. Is able to balance our relationship with other interests
16. Encourages me to feel independent
17. Makes me laugh
18. Respects me

19. Values and cherishes me

20. Makes me feel loved

If you have circled most of these statements, you are most likely involved in a relationship with a compatible partner. If you have not circled many of these items, you may be in an unhealthy relationship and still prone to being in a relationship for all the wrong reasons. It might be time to let this relationship go. You deserve—and will find—someone better.

We live in a time when the options for men and women are almost endless. Many social stigmas are falling away, and as they do, so many possibilities and opportunities have opened up—gay relationships, straight relationships, divorce, living together, living together and having children, pursuing careers, not feeling shame about not getting married, not feeling a responsibility to have children. You have opportunities that your parents and grandparents didn't have. You never have to settle for a relationship that is less than fulfilling.

You also do not have to live in fear that you might be alone forever. With all the dating sites and apps, online meet-ups, and message boards there are almost endless ways to meet someone—a friend, a lover, a partner. *If* that is what you want.

We, Sherry and Beth, wrote this book with a specific intention in our minds. We want to let you know that there is another way. You can break free of your addiction, exorcise the angry ghost of your inner child, and make your own path. Be relaxed, be confident, be fearless. The universe will hold you up. This is the energy we are sending into the universe, the intention we are sending to you.

APPENDIX

The quizzes, questions, and activities you'll find throughout this book are meant to be gentle exercises in self-awareness and healing, not self-criticism. Treat yourself with love and compassion as you do them.

It's also extremely helpful to regularly practice with one or more of the types of exercises you'll find in the chapters. Choose a practice that resonates with you, and you are more likely to stick with it. To help you with your choice, here is some more information about the practices in the book.

POSITIVE AFFIRMATIONS

Affirmations are statements that describe the good things you want to happen in your life. You frame them as a positive statement that is already happening now. Then you repeat them over and over. They're effective because the stories you tell yourself (consciously or unconsciously) are the truths you believe in.

Many people spend a lot of time repeating negative, self-defeating thoughts: "I'm nothing without a partner. I'll never get what I want. I don't deserve love." They keep repeating these negative ideas subconsciously, so even though they're not consciously aware of it, they are accepting them as the truth.

In fact, you can retrain your mind to tell more positive stories. When you do, you are also empowered to take more positive action. Studies have found that interventions designed to help people identify and appreciate their strengths and focus on the positive aspects of their lives can make them happier and decrease depression. Other studies have found that by consciously repeating positive statements about oneself with sincere conviction, people can retrain their minds to think positively. This creates more positive attitudes and reactions, and habits and behaviors that lead to lasting happiness.

Positive affirmations are a tool to consciously change the way you think about yourself and your life. That's because the way you describe something has a huge effect on how you experience it. For instance, if you think of your parents as interfering and nosy, and they call you up and ask, "What did you do this weekend?," you might feel angry because they are not respecting your privacy. If you think of your parents as involved and concerned, and they call you up and ask, "What did you do this weekend?" you might feel cared for because they take a genuine interest in your life. The exact same events, experienced two different ways based on what you believe about your parents.

Along the same lines, imagine you are the kind of person who loses their temper easily. You might tell yourself, "I'm a short-tempered person, there's nothing I can do about that." If that is the story you tell about yourself, you will spend your life losing your temper easily. But if you change the narrative—"I am a tolerant person and slow to anger"—and say it with conviction, as if it's already true, your actions actually start to change. Change your narrative and you change your thinking, and that changes what you do.

Set aside a special time each day, maybe five or ten minutes, when you can repeat your positive affirmations. Repeat them with conviction and purpose. However, it's important to remember that you can't just repeat your positive affirmations once or twice a day and then spend the rest of the day in a spiral of negative thoughts. So also repeat them whenever those negative thoughts start to creep in. When you repeat your affirmations, close your eyes, breathe deeply through your nose, and imagine all the positive things that are already on their way. Thank the universe as if you already have these things.

Here are some positive affirmations you might find useful on your journey.

I am a loveable and valuable person.

I deserve a healthy partner who is capable of loving, respecting, and honoring me.

My needs and wants are important.

All my experiences contribute to my growth.

I am learning to let go of dependence on others and rely on myself for happiness.

I attract loving people.

I create my own truth in love.

You may find that at different times in your life you need to remind yourself of different things. It's easy to create your own positive affirmations, based on what you need to bring into your life. What's most important when creating positive affirmations is not to come from a place of lack, but instead from a place where you already have received what you desire. That's why it is important to use statements that declare that what you want is already happening—"I am" types of statements, rather than those that start with "I want" or "I need." Positive affirmations should be just that—positive. You are creating statements of what you desire in your life, rather than what you are avoiding or no longer want. "I am a person who deserves a healthy relationship" is much more powerful then saying, "I no longer want to be obsessed with my ex-boyfriend."

If you have trouble visualizing what it is you want, picture yourself three years from now, as if you have all those things you desire. Imagine running into an old friend. What would you want to share with them about your new life? Write those things down as if they are happening right now. Write them in the present tense.

Your positive affirmations will be more effective and you will feel more empowered when your affirmations come from not only your thoughts but also your feelings. When you write them, write in your authentic voice—the inner voice where truth lives. Write them with passion and desire. Notice in your core what it will feel like when you accomplish these goals.

There are no rules about writing your positive affirmations in terms of how many you write or how long they should be (although make sure they are short enough that you can easily remember them). What's most important is that they reflect you and what it is you want to experience, wish to manifest, and would like to transform.

You can also write positive affirmations about the things you are already grateful for in your life. It is extremely powerful to say, "I am so happy and grateful that . . ." By doing this, you teach your mind to focus on the positive instead of the negative. You might say, "I have a great job," or "My friends are supportive," or "My pet loves me unconditionally." This increases the positive vibrations you are putting out into the universe, allowing the universe to attract back to you your truest desires.

Remember, you can't think your way to positive feelings; you must feel your way to more empowering thoughts. It is the positive feeling states you embody that will bring you all you desire in your relationships and in your life.

Having a relationship, however, is not the end goal. We all know plenty of people who are lonely or miserable in their relationships because they don't have the trust, security, support, respect, or intimacy they long for. Let go of the goal that you must find someone to be in a relationship with, and instead use your affirmations to feel how a vital, healthy, nurturing, supportive relationship might feel. Just remember that the relationship is not going to bring you the positive feeling states. It is the positive feeling states that are going to bring you self-love, which opens up the possibility of a healthy relationship—or not. You know you will be okay either way.

MINDFULNESS

Mindfulness means being fully in the present moment. Jon Kabat-Zinn describes it as "paying attention, in a particular way, on purpose, in the present moment, and nonjudgmentally." That means paying conscious attention to what you are doing, what you are saying, what you are feeling, and what you are thinking.

The opposite of mindfulness is reacting out of impulse, functioning on autopilot, falling into habitual patterns of thinking, worrying about the future, or being concerned about the past. Often people follow unconscious patterns of thought and behavior that are familiar and therefore require less effort. When you're not consciously aware of those thoughts and behaviors, you fall into the same damaging patterns again and again.

The Buddhists say that our lives are an illusion. What they mean by that is not that the real world is an illusion, but that we spend most of our lives paying attention to everything except the real world. How many times have you spent minutes or even hours doing something you later can't remember doing, with your mind chattering away about something that, in retrospect, you don't even recall? When you begin your mindfulness practice, you will be surprised to discover how much of your life—both inner thoughts and feelings and outer words and actions—happens on autopilot.

A lot of research has been done into the ways mindfulness can improve people's lives. Neuroscientists have shown that practicing mindfulness increases the brain's grey matter, which is the part of the brain responsible for making decisions, focusing and keeping attention, solving problems, and moderating behavior. It also decreases activity in the amygdala, the part of the brain that responds to emotional triggers and physical threats.

Something as simple as taking a few deep, slow breaths and focusing on the here and now activates the parasympathetic nervous system. That's the part of the involuntary nervous system that conserves energy by slowing down the heart rate, increasing intestinal and glandular activity, and relaxing the sphincter muscles in the gastrointestinal tract. The response is sometimes called "rest and digest"—the opposite of "fight or flight."

Mindfulness training has also been shown to reduce stress and to help people think more clearly and remain calm and focused in stressful situations. It also helps people become more aware of the content of their thoughts and feelings and better able to distinguish between what is a thought or feeling or worry and what is actually happening in their lives.

Being mindful takes practice. You'll have to remind yourself throughout the day to stop, notice what you are doing, and really be present in the moment. To start, pick a few tasks you do every day—say, brushing your teeth—and work on paying attention to that task and nothing else. Notice the feeling of your toothbrush on your teeth and gums, the flavor of the toothpaste, the temperature of the water when you rinse your mouth. What do you do with your lips, tongue, hands? Don't think about anything else. If you notice your mind wandering, just bring your attention back to brushing your teeth.

You can be attentive in this same way when you wash the dishes, take a shower, or eat your lunch. Pay attention solely to what you are doing. Focus on your senses—the sights, sounds, tastes, and smells—and the physical sensations of your experience. Notice when your mind wanders to thoughts, judgments, assumptions, and expectations, and when you revert to automatic behaviors. Just bring yourself back to the present moment, without judgment.

A good way to remind yourself to be mindful throughout the day is to set your phone timer to go off every ninety minutes. When it does, stop, take a few deep breaths, and center yourself in the present moment.

These very simple exercises have a powerful purpose. As you practice mindfulness, you'll get better and better at distinguishing what is real in your life from the stories you are telling yourself. You will become less reactive, less stressed. You'll respond less on autopilot and more from a place of thoughtful consideration. You'll begin to see how much the voice in your head has been running the show, and where that voice is coming from. If it's the voice of your wounded inner child or your relationship addiction, you'll be able to recognize that. When you recognize those voices, you'll be able to quiet them and listen instead to the voice of your inner wisdom.

MEDITATION

Meditation is one of the tools you can use to become more mindful. Just about every moment that you're awake, your mind is chattering away. It's judging everything you see, hear, and do—including you. It's reliving the past—either feeling nostalgic for it or trying to rewrite it. It's jumping into the future—worrying about something that may never happen, fantasizing about alternate scenarios. It's making up conversations and encounters, setting up appointments, creating shopping lists, or picking out bridesmaids for your fantasy wedding. Even when you're doing something designed to grab your attention, like listening to music, watching a movie, or having a conversation, your mind is jumping from past to present to future, from reality to fantasy, all the time.

Experienced meditators call this monkey mind, and even they must constantly deal with that monkey who endlessly chatters and hops around. Meditation is a way to calm the monkey mind, turn off all the chatter, and give yourself a break from that endless stream of judgment. Meditators strive for a state of thoughtless awareness—being aware of the present moment without thinking about it any way.

Meditation has been extensively studied by both medical doctors and psychologists, and its benefits have been documented in numerous studies. If you Google "What are the benefits of meditation?" more answers will appear than we can possibly list here. That's why large corporations, hospitals, and universities, among others, are officially sponsoring meditation groups for their employees.

The physical benefits include slowed aging because of changes in brain physiology, and improvements in a host of health problems, including high blood pressure, sleep disturbances, gastrointestinal distress, headaches, chronic pain, and skin disorders. The psychological benefits include reduced stress, improved concentration, a greater sense of calm, increased self-awareness, increased happiness, and increased acceptance of your life, yourself, and others, Meditation induces relaxation, which benefits both cardiovascular and immune health. It can help relieve mild depression, reduce obsessive thinking, and encourage optimism.

It's very easy to begin a meditation practice. To start, set aside ten minutes a day. As you become better at meditation, you'll want to add more time. Increase the time as you desire it; don't push yourself, or else you won't do it all. Sit comfortably upright in a quiet room. Set a silent timer (such as your phone) for ten minutes. Adjust your body so you will not have to move at all for your whole meditation session.

Now, gently close your eyes and direct your focus to a single, simple thing. It might be the sensation of your breath going in and out. It might be a word or sound you repeat to yourself. If you decide to focus this way, choose a word that has no meaning, or one with a neutral meaning, so you do not get caught up in any emotional associations with the word. For example, you might say "soooo" as you breathe in and "hahhhhhh" as you breathe out. Or you can use numbers—"one" as you breathe in and "two" as you breathe out. You can say these words out loud, or you can just say them to yourself.

You can also focus on a particular image or experience for your meditation. For example, as you breathe in and breathe out, feel the connection between your mind, your body, and your spirit. With every inhale imagine you are taking in nourishing golden energy. The healing properties of this golden energy are filling up every cell of your body with love and light. With every exhale, imagine you are releasing all that no longer is serving you—all the fear, worries, anxiety, thoughts, beliefs, and emotions that keep you feeling small. Imagine this dark energy of negativity flowing from the room you are sitting in, out the window, and out into the universe with each exhale. Allow yourself to receive love, light, peace, serenity, compassion, and joy from the universe with each inhale.

Try to focus on nothing but your breath or your words or images. But know that everyone, even very experienced meditators, has monkey mind. When you sense your mind wandering, just gently bring it back to the object of your focus. Don't judge yourself, don't get angry or frustrated, and don't stop. Just come back and keep meditating. The practice of mediation is not sitting for ten minutes with an empty mind; it's sitting for ten minutes and noticing when the mind is running off track, then gently bringing it back.

Eventually you will find that meditation opens up a quiet space for wisdom to emerge. That might happen because when you finally silence your monkey mind, even for a few seconds, your wiser self can finally be heard. Or you might notice that your monkey mind keeps jumping to a few particular places. In meditation, you can be detached from these thoughts and examine what they are. Does your monkey constantly jump to feelings of negativity, lack, or emptiness? When you're aware of this, rather than it happening in the background of your subconscious, you can begin to consciously guide your thoughts to more positive places. (Positive affirmations can be helpful for this.) You can gently quiet the monkey, sort out reality from the endless chatter, and begin to reframe the stories you tell yourself about your life.

GUIDED VISUALIZATIONS

Guided visualization is a form of meditation; it's also sometimes called guided mediation, guided imagery, or yoga nidra. While the purpose of meditation is to quiet your mind and make you aware of your automatic thoughts, guided visualization takes you on a specific journey. Depending on the visualization, it may be designed to help you reflect on important questions, release a particular anger or negative energy, or heal old wounds.

Guided imagery taps into the fact that your body and mind are connected. When you focus on imagining something, your body responds as if what you are imagining is real. If you are imagining yourself eating an apple, for example—the color, the smell, the crisp texture, the flavor—you actually salivate. If you imagine you are someplace safe, comfortable, and relaxing, your body responds similarly, letting go of tension and fear.

Research has found that guided visualization can have many of the same benefits as meditation. It may lower blood pressure, boost immune cell activity, promote healing, lessen pain and headaches, accelerate weight loss, reduce anxiety, and help people cope with the effects of chemotherapy. It can also heighten positive emotions, spirituality, intuition, abstract thinking, and empathy. And because it mobilizes unconscious processes in the mind to assist with conscious goals, it can boost motivation and gather resources to help you accomplish what you desire.

Guided visualization has the power to reach your subconscious mind. It creates powerful imagined journeys that your brain then experiences as real. When you have a real experience, new neural pathways are formed within the brain, and when you listen to a guided visualization, you can also rewire your brain to form new neural pathways. One great advantage of guided visualization is that if you fall asleep, you still benefit subconsciously from the experience.

In a guided visualization, you sit or lie down and listen to a recorded narrator. It may last as little as fifteen minutes or as long as fifty. You can download or buy CDs, a meditation app, or listen to guided visualizations online. You can also find scripts in books or online that you record yourself and play back for your meditation, or you can write your own guided visualization. (Some people don't like the sound of their own voice and ask a trusted friend to record a guided visualization for them.)

The meditation will direct you to imagine yourself in a particular place or situation, or on a journey. You may imagine yourself on a beach or in a forest. Or you may visualize yourself as bathed in healing light or supported by nurturing beings. Different journeys are designed for different purposes; there are guided visualizations for relaxation, for realizing your goals, for getting rid of bad habits and addictions, for healing old wounds, and many others. You will probably find that you need different ones at different times.

JOURNALING

Far more than simply a diary, journaling is a tool to help you get back in touch with your authentic self and explore the ideas in your conscious and subconscious mind. It's the simplest way to open the door to who you really are; that authentic person who is longing to be more, do more, and of course, heal your relationship addiction. It can help you bring into focus your hopes and fears, uncover your hidden life story, and peel back the layers of your self that you have never allowed yourself to see.

Journaling also enables you to recognize and discard those belief systems in your life that are no longer serving you. Journaling about traumatic events can help you explore them and release the emotions associated with them. It can help you pinpoint what is no longer working in your life, including toxic relationships, get past your addictive behaviors, and explore the questions and answers that are the foundation of your belief system.

While journaling has been practiced for hundreds and perhaps thousands of years, it's only been studied very recently by scientists. They've found that it can clarify thoughts and feelings, reduce stress, boost the immune system, help you know yourself better, solve problems more effectively, and resolve disagreements with others.

To get started, buy yourself a notebook and a pen that you'll use just for journaling. Buy yourself things you really like; consider the design of the cover, the weight and texture of the paper, the color and flow of the pen. Set aside a time each day to journal in a place where it is quiet and peaceful, and those who live with you will respect your privacy and alone time. Maybe tuck yourself under a comforter, or light a candle, or put on some special music. If you feel more creative or energized around others, the local coffee shop or a park or beach can also be a great place to journal. Create a space and a ritual that works for you.

Journaling does not even have to be expressed in written words. You can draw, paint, doodle, or whatever resonates with your creativity, your happiness, and your pain. There is no right or wrong way to journal. Just keep it simple and do what feels right for you.

Write a date at the top of the page and just get started. Write anything that comes to mind—even if it's not complete sentences, even if it's nonsense. Don't think about your grammar or punctuation or spelling. Write for at least ten minutes, and don't worry if what you write keeps jumping from subject to subject. The goal is to have a place to write where there are no barriers; where your inner voice can express itself on paper without negative voices critiquing you. It's about honoring your process, not the journal itself. Write quickly and don't edit or cross things out. The point here is to silence your internal editor. Let go and allow the spirit of exploration to be part of your journaling.

Do something calming for a few minutes after you finish writing. Then come back and read what you just wrote. Try to understand what your inner, unedited voice is trying to convey. Write a sentence or two at the bottom of your entry that describes the insight you've gained from journaling today.

You want to write regularly, allowing all of life to show up in your journal. When you review your journal entries at a later date, you will realize that pain is temporary and that there is an ebb and flow to your emotions. The idea is to see the patterns in your life, including your toxic relationships and the cycle of those relationships. It helps you gain perspective, so that you can make changes in these patterns. And remember, journaling is a journey, not a destination.

This kind of journaling is open-ended and is intended to help you get in touch with thoughts and feelings you have been pushing away or simply have not had the time to examine. But it can also be helpful to journal with a particular question in mind. We have posed many questions for you throughout this book, and all of them are excellent topics to explore in your journal.

Alternatively, you might consider keeping an accomplishment journal. This is a place to celebrate your accomplishments each day with gratitude. Rather than focusing on the negative, you are focusing on the positive. This shifts your consciousness to what's right in your life instead of what's wrong—and can even help retrain your brain to concentrate on the good rather than the bad in your life.

Each morning and night jot down at least one accomplishment for the day.

One accomplishment today that I acknowledge and rejoice in is_____.

It could be as simple as *I acknowledge and rejoice in the fact that I called a trusted friend instead of texting my ex today. I acknowledge and rejoice in the fact that I joined a support group for relationship addicts. I acknowledge and rejoice in the fact that I practiced self-care today.*

Every day, read over your accomplishments for the previous few days. Then begin to observe how your focus on gratitude rather than lack affects your relationship addiction, rewires your brain for more positivity, and gives you new joy, new insights, and new understanding. As you celebrate your life, you begin to attract healthier relationships with people who are also filled with gratitude and joy.

It is important to keep your journal private. Journaling is a place to share your most sacred feelings safely and unselfconsciously. However, you may decide at some point that sharing your deepest feelings is a calling to support others in their journey. In that case, starting a blog can be very healing and helpful to others.

CPSIA information can be obtained
at www.ICGtesting.com
Printed in the USA
LVHW031351240322
714285LV00010B/483